The Garden in Every Sense and Season

The Garden in Every Sense and Season

TOVAH MARTIN

PHOTOGRAPHS BY KINDRA CLINEFF

TIMBER PRESS
PORTLAND, OREGON

CONTENTS

Introduction: *Coming to My Senses* 7

SPRING

SUMMER

AUTUMN

WINTER

INTRODUCTION

Coming to My Senses

THIS IS THE story of a nose and how I followed it through the year. This is the saga of a garden and how it spoke to me. In these pages I chronicle a pair of hands as they grope their way through the weeding, hoeing, and digging without too much pain. And this is the tale of someone who has looked at her garden for years, but only now saw it fully for the first time. I have learned that unless you consciously experience your garden, you might be blind to its beauty. And if you don't listen, it will remain mute. This is the journal of an awakening told throughout the course of a year. But it is not my individual story—it is everyone's.

What is it about gardening? So often, it's like a tsunami, and we are caught up in its rush until we drown. Not only do we go under, but we are submerged without any of the deep-rooted memories that made martyrdom worth the sacrifice. We tend to forget that the garden is a very close, personal relationship, and we don't stroke it enough.

I was that person. I was the weed warrior with the gimlet eye focused solely on stray chickweed and opportunistic witch grass. I was blind and I

(FOLLOWING PAGES) Doesn't every gardener utter the same lament? We get so wrapped up in the wheelbarrowing, we forget to savor the experience.

was deaf. I felt the sting of the rose—which I cluelessly placed by the front door—tearing my flesh while I juggled the flat of plants, the keys, and my knapsack. I grew the paperwhites in winter, which offended my nostrils in close quarters after dark. I experienced a few spare moments of awakening, but I also made senseless mistakes because of numbness. This is the frantic response of the frenetic gardener.

I call my seven acres Furthermore because I'm continually over-extending. My mind races ahead of physical reality and, before I know it, another project is in the works and I'm galloping to make it happen. When I came to this land in northwestern Connecticut, nothing botanical was in residence save a few struggling irises around the foundation. I asked 95-year-old Mabel Smith whether a garden ever resided here when the land was still part of her family farm. She pointed to the front yard with her shaky cane and responded, "A garden? Of course there was a garden! A potato patch was planted right here." So there you have it. I am returning this property to its glorious roots.

I came in 1996, and over the years I have inserted a garden to spread in front of the 1790 cottage (converted into living space from a former cobbler's shop), put in an herb-vegetable garden behind the house, installed a berry garden and a massive vegetable garden, and upcycled what was left of the front lawn into a lawn-alternative garden. I've planted dozens and dozens of trees. I steward an acre of New England meadow, diversifying it slightly from the original mono-goldenrod inventory to include other natives such as Joe Pye weed, pycnanthemum, and numerous asters. I built a barn for my two Saanen goats, and they graze placidly (sometimes) in their paddock—all the while keeping an eye peeled for devilry to wreak if I leave a gate unguarded for half a second. Inside the house and its attached converted barn, Einstein (a shelter kitten whose lineage includes mischievous Maine Coon) watches from various windows. More than 200 plants reside in the house in the colder months, to be liberated outdoors to various porches and patios when weather permits. Furthermore is the stage where my ultimate revelation took place. It provides ample fodder for feeling—if only I was wired that way. This is my journey of sensory illumination.

The idea for this book came from you. During lectures, I often begin by asking my audience to close their eyes and pull up a sensation. And you wouldn't believe where we go from that simple prompting. We return to childhood. We talk about jasmines floating into windows and the seductive aroma of freshly mown grass. Afterward, we know each other a little better. And we see opportunities that we were blind to while careening around. Gardeners are kin—fellow diggers in the dirt—and we are kindled. As a result of my sensory awakening, I love Furthermore even more today. I'm hoping to ignite that sort of deeper relationship in you.

Through my lectures I have learned that our perceptions are universally shared. We like similar sensations. Lots of us have color preferences. And we have other commonalities—for example, who doesn't want to avoid injuries? But do you analyze tools before purchasing them, or just go for the handsomest presentation? We tend toward tunnel vision. We sometimes forget to plug in all our senses, and the garden is diluted as a result. We rush out with our tool trug in hand and get down to business. We rip and tear with all our might to create the sensational garden of our dreams, and then we forget to experience those sensations. We don't plug in.

This adventure could be so multilayered. The garden has so much potential. If only we would take time to do the 360-degree turn and gather all the stimuli, just think how much more fruitful our garden might become. We have a uniquely privileged viewpoint. The glistening hues of tree peony flowers, the shine of light as it illuminates leaves, the velvety touch of lamb's ears, the buzz of pollinators as they go about their duties, the flit of birds as they make use of what we have offered to further the survival of their species—they are all part of the privilege. Tasting the salty sweat, listening to the chink of the hoe as it dispatches the weeds, touching our hands to the Braille of statuary or just wrapping our fingers around a clot of our own homegrown soil—it's all ours to savor. We are cheating ourselves if we don't perk up.

So it's time. Now is the right moment to build on the cues that have accumulated over the years and listen up, look over, inhale, savor, and reach out. Come and join me. Explore your garden through the seasons for all it's worth. Become attuned.

Spring

Couldn't you just hug it? Don't you want to embrace every single branch that bravely leafs out in defiance of the cruel winter it survived? Spring is the welcome-back season. It's the sweet nectar we have been anticipating through all those months of waiting. But it's also the time of year when we suffer the worst case of tunnel vision of the calendar. Spring is a relay race, and we act like the sprinters.

Spring is an outpouring of tender nubile growth just bristling with promise that is exciting to all the senses.

IN THE RUSH to run out and get your hands dirty, sometimes you forget to savor spring. The garden is crying for its layer of compost before the perennials sprout up. But prior to tackling that chore, you need to rake all those leaves that scuttled in to cling around the spireas. And where did all those twigs littering the lawn come from? The evergreen boughs placed in window boxes looked clever bravely poking out from the snow, but now they seem pitiful. The deer fencing that protected your arborvitae now strikes the eye with all the grace of a construction site. The peonies need to be fitted with supports before they sprout. You have to send the soil out for testing. The compost needs to be fetched. I could continue, but you're already sweating bullets.

Meanwhile, there is so much to see and hear and touch in spring. The first taste of your own produce is melt-in-your-mouth delicious. The spring pageant of flowers is a particularly proud moment. You need to stop and admire all these rewards. That tree peony is going to pop, but it will remain open for only a few days. If we get a spring cloudburst (and the odds are good), it might soon be hanging its head with the burden of soggy petals. And the distinctive color combinations that coincide today might be gone tomorrow if the tulips are shattered in a storm or the temperatures climb to cut short the columbine's glory. And speaking of columbines, did you hear the first hummingbirds as they flew in for the unfolding of those flowers? Were you listening for the first call of the red-winged blackbirds? While you were working, did you groove to the music of your tools?

Your garden is honking on all levels, so take heed. Wallow in the fruits of your labor while they are happening. Once you begin to perceive, you learn things you never knew. Maybe that ugly stump fallen into decay is somebody's home. Maybe that tangle of brush has a nest. Maybe that chance seedling is the happiest color accident that ever crossed your path. Maybe you need a bench just to enjoy it all. Maybe you need to actually sit on that bench. Just an idea.

Sight

SPRING GREEN

Y OU GOBBLE UP spring in one bite, but you anticipate its coming for an eternity. Spring is slow food for your senses. If ever there was a season that we fabricate from thin air, it's spring. I envision spring's arrival long before the first hints appear. Isn't the grass just a tad greener than it was yesterday? Do I see tiny signs of life on the tips of blueberry branches that were nothing but smooth, unpromising brown sticks a week ago? Because spring is more a dream than a reality for an extended period of time, it seems way too long in coming. If wishing would make it true, spring would be in full-blown splendor the day after it is announced on the calendar. But maybe the slow, sweet seduction is a better idea.

Spring starts as a series of subtle hints in a visual treasure hunt. The grass begins sending up tentative green blades where before it was just a sickly, flaxen, trampled mat. Magnolia buds swell into plumpness and threaten to burst open even though frost is predicted. *Iris cristata* breaks the surface of the ground, brandishing buds; crocuses unfold to a revelry of famished bees; pussy willows line the stream banks. All those presumptuous little plants that pop up prematurely in spring are like life rafts. Without the lungwort, I don't know where I'd be. But I see it as hope rather than a promise. When the trees are finally crowned in a veil of green, that's the definitive moment. Is the tulip poplar really showing leaf buds? Are buds swelling on the forsythia? Is the crabapple coloring up in yonder tree grove? Do I see a flowering quince emanating a little halo of chartreuse? Fingers crossed.

That sort of optimism continues for most of April, until finally one day it's definitely true. Spring is a great argument for leaving some woodland surrounding your property because that's where the green first gets a foothold and gains enough momentum to inspire hope. You look out on that compendium of trees (there is strength in numbers) and, sure enough, tender spring green is really visible, even to the doubters. The white birch blushes verdant combined with its rust-colored dangling tassels. The sugar maples are clothed in their catkins. On your drives, you

view Impressionistic pointillism through windshield wipers batting away at the inevitable sprinkles of rain. Pinks and burnished oranges make a broadloom with nubile chartreuse. Everything is full of promise; everything is quivering with come-hither vibes. Spring is incredibly sexy.

Before it is officially spring, the vining honeysuckles form tentative leaves so precocious that their brazen tips are frequently nipped in the frost. They'll revive anew. Not long afterward, the rugosa roses stud their prickly stems with initial pleated leaves. They will also survive a frost or

---

Most shrubs and trees turn forest green later in spring, but their first tender leaves emerge a sparkling shade of chartreuse.

two. The ninebark is among the first shrubs to show color (much to the delight of newly arriving birds, who seize the opportunity to feed), followed by the Japanese maples. Tree peonies form leaf clusters improbably crowning the tips of what look like blanched cigar stems. The equally unpoetic tiger eye sumac is not far on their heels with its tawny first leaves. What seemed so wretchedly forlorn weeks ago springs into action with the kiss of increasing light. It's like magic. No wonder we are all bursting with spring fever.

It's not really about us, of course—we are merely the sideline cheerleaders. Everything has an ulterior motive. Nature designed it so the tiger eye sumac sprouts only from the tips, leaving gnarled denuded branches laid bare. Those naked branches are perfectly suited for the labors of nest-building finches. The lilacs are equally hasty to arrive on the scene, followed immediately by their clusters of buds that mature into flowers in a flash. Grow these shrubs just to feast your eyes after a season of dearth. You deserve that leafy morale boost from the rugosa rose.

Other things are happening farther afield. Traitors are revealing their true colors. Before anything else greens up, the barberry exposes its villainous self in the woods, making the invasive nuisance an easy target for removal. Ditto for the equally nefarious multiflora rose. Get out there and vanquish them before you become preoccupied with spring cleanup.

These plants lead the charge of the light brigade. Later, the viburnums will finally prove that they survived the winter. And the beautyberry will leave you guessing far too long before it shows any signs of life. But I really yearn for the spireas. They are certainly not first on the agenda, but their early spring pageant of frisky color hues spells spring for many a color-famished gardener. Sprinkle in some columbine (have you met *Aquilegia canadensis* 'Little Lanterns'?), with *Geum* 'Bell Bank' or 'Flames of Passion' lapping at its ankles, and you have something truly heart-stopping. In fact, you could stuff in the pansies by the trailer load. But that comes later, when you take the first rustlings of chartreuse and run with them. What starts with a simple hint of green expands into no-holds-barred excess. Arresting is what spring is meant to be. Later, green will become the framework of the garden. Green will designate the boundaries with hedges and create the arches, forming the defining moments when it gathers gumption. But it all begins with a pale green suggestion. Take note and take heart.

NOT-SO-MELLOW YELLOWS

S PRING IS NO season for the faint of heart, on any level. It bursts. It throbs. It reverberates with the affirmation of life. It's all about purposeful excess. If we're going to have a growing season, spring has to hit the ground running. So it makes perfect sense that yellow predominates in spring.

I often wonder if we would welcome the startling yellows of spring at any other time of year. Think about the ocean of acrid winter aconite that floods any scene where one bulb has been planted, or marsh marigold that sneaks in to stud a garden with gold. But spring isn't just underfoot. I wait impatiently for the fluffy yellow blossoms on *Cornus officinalis*. Every morning, I check the progress of that blooming dogwood similar to *C. mas*, but with sexier bark. Every evening I shine the flashlight on its burden of plump buds in the hopes that a few are showing their strident yellow inner workings. When they start to burst, it's the sounding bell— the Yellow Tide has officially begun. And the effusive yellow forsythia is not far behind. In summer, we threaten to banish those ill-kempt shrubs with a mind of their own and a look-at-me spring flash that was undoubtedly the inspiration behind school buses. But come spring, we count the moments until they open. Forsythias are in a showmanship competition with the legions of blaring yellow 'Carlton', 'Dutch Master', and 'Marieke' daffodils that trumpet the charge of spring. Every year, breeders introduce more muted shades of peach, cream, and white daffodils. But I'm willing to bet that the traditional yellows eclipse them all in sales.

Admit it, you crave yellow. You crane your neck to see if the jonquils have burst open overnight. While you're bouncing around country roads, your kids' noses are pressed to the window of the car, counting daffodils. You hope they'll be open for Easter. You plant the varieties that will read bright and cheerful from the street. Spring has its own set of color rules.

I've heard gardeners bash yellow. At other times of year, people say unkind things about the color. Some folks even claim to avoid it entirely in their landscapes. I'd like to go on record as not being a member of that particular faction of the NIMBY (not in my backyard) movement. Yellow

is the pollen guide in the throat of many flowers (like pansies) that directs pollinators to their payload. Many flowers have yellow somewhere in their configuration, serving as a unifying theme. Throughout the year, I accent my garden with the full complement of yellow coreopsis, yarrow, and anthemis. That said, in high summer I tone it down. I tend to veer toward butter, blonde, or cadmium. These shades play better with their neighbors, and they don't require sunglasses for viewing.

Cornus officinalis beats the forsythia in my garden, opening its lacy yellow blossoms as one of the earliest harbingers of spring.

You have to give each season its own specific slack. I explain my open-minded color policy in spring as the simple desire to get outside and embrace nature again. When spring has settled down, I tend to select a pink evening primrose rather than the stark yolk-colored version. Only in spring would I opt for bright canary primroses rather than a more demure shade. But spring needs to make a statement, and yellow is a good ambassador.

The other day, I saw a combination of tulips and daffodils that read like a three-alarm fire from a distance. I'm not sure if it would be such a welcome sight in midsummer. But in spring, I say bring it on. Bring on the fury, the flaming shades, the indiscreet colors. Namby-pamby can come later.

SPIREAS: GREAT BALLS OF FIRE

CONFESSION: MY GARDEN verges on too racy in spring. Some people might find it appalling. You should turn the page and move on to another topic if (1) you have any tendencies toward being buttoned-down, (2) your garden style is limited to only shades of green, (3) you are prone to pooh-poohing gardens of color. On these seven acres, spring is about packing it in. For example, given a choice between a green boxwood ball and a clipped spirea, I would opt for the spirea in a heartbeat. Call me trashy, but I like my garden vibrant in spring.

In the garden, carefree abandon translates into stacks of spirea orbs with columbines, geum, and spring-blooming bulbs wading beneath them. Throw in a few tree and herbaceous peonies to break up the textural motif, and you have a quick summary of what happens here in spring. Actually, spring starts in autumn when I give my spireas the first of many buzz cuts. Although the garden is lusty in spring, it is not disheveled. At least, the spireas and a few other shrubs are a brave attempt to impose some clean, sharp lines on the place. Basically, as soon as I get home from

traveling and during any spare moment when I'm not weeding or otherwise engaged, I am wielding shears and clipping away at my spireas. There is no danger of these shrubs scattering seed (which they can do—too prolifically, I'm told) because they hardly get a chance to bloom, let alone be fruitful. Procreation isn't in their future.

Spireas are all about color, which is delivered in the leaves as well as flowers (if you let them blossom, which I don't). I have *Spiraea japonica* 'Gold Mound', 'Gold Flame', 'Magic Carpet', and several others, and I stagger their heights to achieve the layering I love. Like other people

Thank goodness the spireas form mounds to punctuate the garden with structure.

do boxwood orbs, I work on my spireas. 'Gold Flame' and 'Magic Carpet' give me the orange new growth that works with the columbine and geum fetish. Scatter a few *Aquilegia* 'Origami Red and White' between some little round 'Magic Carpet' balls, and who wouldn't be in heaven? This year, I found toadflax to add to the vision. It keeps pumping out little snapdragon-like magenta-and-yellow blossoms throughout the season. Meanwhile, 'Magic Carpet' will calm down and turn green-gold after the kick-up-your-heels season is over. It will step back to form the repetitive sentinel sense of shape in the garden. That's a good thing, because summer and autumn have their own agendas, and I need the spireas to let those shows get under way.

Not everyone wants spring to be loud. For pastel people, spireas might not be the way to go. You can clip away at your boxwoods and tsk disapprovingly when you drive by (my garden is pretty much out there on the road), and I'll do my thing at Furthermore. Discretion and I parted company long ago. Nowadays, I don't really care what anybody else thinks. Editors can snip away at my manuscripts, restaurants can tell me that I have to change from my garden rags in order to dine, but my garden is my own domain. You are welcome to take a similar stance toward your yardage. It seems far more important that the finches like what we've done. And yes, I have found nests hidden in the lower branches of my densely clipped spirea orbs. After all, it isn't really all about us.

TRUE BLUE

TRUE BLUE ISN'T often found in the garden. In the natural realm, cobalt blossoms are scarce. Instead, we usually get purples and mauves. But not in spring. This is the season when all the azure, indigo, cerulean, and sailor shades come out of the closet.

The grass has just turned from brown to green when the blues start creeping in. In my neighborhood, it begins with *Scilla siberica* 'Spring

Beauty'. Years ago, someone with a whole lot of vision started a tentative scilla patch at the main intersection in town. The current homeowner nurtures it faithfully, and over many years it has grown from a puddle into a small ocean. The scillas stand only a few inches tall, so one or two would never make a statement. Even several dozen would faze no one. But now that their numbers have reached swarm proportions of many hundreds of thousands, they take the scene by storm. My neighbor reportedly requests that her husband refrain from mowing the yard until after the seeds have ripened and strewn themselves around. The mowing lapse requires only a few weeks, and the grass never gets shaggy. Seems like a small investment to achieve such a traffic-stopper.

I stage another type of blue moment. Occasionally, my muscari and hyacinths overlap. Rather than the hybrid hyacinths with their fat foxtail spikes, I prefer the loose *Hyacinthus orientalis* 'Festival' types with multiple stems that are less densely packed. The blues are magnificent, and they strike a nearly wild note. Combine them with grape hyacinths, which are stridently periwinkle or approaching turquoise (if you grow *Muscari armeniacum* 'Valerie Finnis'), and you have a rhapsody in blue. Meanwhile, I see the open-faced pale blue blossoms of *Chionodoxa forbesii* rushing around. Even in a late snow (God forbid), their spirit and stems never seem to get crushed. Chionodoxa is such a wise investment in spring, even if you're not the gambling type. A little later, the camassias will follow. Their hue is more in the purple range, but en masse it still reads as blue from a distance.

It's not just about bulbs. In my garden, the lungworts are totally precocious. I know you've seen the long spotted leaves spread out close to the ground—they are very hard to miss, even when not flowering. In spring, they scarcely pop out of the ground before they burst into blossom. The pink *Pulmonaria* 'Raspberry Splash' opens first, but *P. saccharata* 'Mrs. Moon' follows close on its heels with an eclipse of light blue blossoms. Fortunately, 'Mrs. Moon' is undaunted by late frosts or a light layer of snow. You need that sort of foot soldier in April. And you also desperately need a dose of the color pulmonaria delivers.

Other blues make their debut in early spring. There is woodland phlox creeping along the ground waving a pale blue banner over its head.

Iris reticulata is one of the first bulbs to pop up and perform in earliest spring, and 'Harmony' is described as bluebird blue, which is pretty accurate. Navy blue *Primula vulgaris* hybrids infuse shaded areas with a color that seems almost surreal. I grow a little swarm of blue *P. denticulata* beneath my black walnut, and those drumstick primroses thumb their noses at the toxins that the walnuts send into the soil. *Primula denticulata* is actually purple, but it's close enough. Plant a colony of primroses, and it will entertain the next seven generations.

Grape hyacinth makes other blues appear purple in comparison.

Later in spring, *Salvia ×sylvestris* 'Rhapsody in Blue' will open its spires in a color that is considerably brighter and more vibrant than the deep navy of most *S. nemorosa* hybrids. The dark shade of 'May Night' and 'New Dimension Blue' fail to read from a distance and can appear more like a dark hole than a bouncy hue. But by the time they arrive at the party, the first electric blues of spring are only a happy memory, and the garden has settled into more conservative shades. Don't you love the way that works?

Smell

EARTH

Spring sneaks in through a crack in the window. It steals in when you push the panes open for that whiff of fresh air you've anticipated for so long. You've almost forgotten what the mingling of indoors and outside feels like; it's been an eternity since you bonded. But then the scent of warm soil slips through the thin crack in the slightly ajar window. It is deep, rich, and sexy. It's primal. It's earthy. It makes you want to run outside, get down on hands and knees, gather a fistful, and inhale. You want to dig in, you want to give it a hug, you want to welcome it back. And you realize how much you missed that scent for too many long, lean months.

It will appear on your radar in other interludes. You might be walking down the street, lost in thought, and suddenly you'll be touched by a gentle breeze petting your cheek. A discreet scent floats by, and you recognize that aroma as your old friend, the newly thawed soil.

That singular scent is lost to your senses later in the season. At least, my nose becomes immune to it. It's the smell of all those micro-organisms waking, all that humus getting ready for action, all those sprouts revving up. Perfumers have told me that the smell of freshly baked bread is the universal favorite aroma that supersedes citrus, vanilla, and other aromatic crowd-pleasers. My own informal polling has revealed that the smell of warming earth is the people's choice for gardeners. It doesn't make our tummies rumble, but it does put a little Mona Lisa smile on our lips. It's laden with all sorts of welcome baggage. For a gardener, there's a strong association with good things to come, like lettuce and columbines.

Later in the season, when spring is in full swing, your nose is barraged by other stimuli. It has to answer calls coming in through a switchboard that's wildly lighting up on all circuits. Your nose is distracted by scents that aren't nearly as subtle. For example, you get eau de amendments

---

Plenty of bare soil is available to smell when the peonies first emerge.

coming in loud and clear—amendments, of course, is a euphemism for compost and various other fertilizers.

Beyond putting your nose to the air and savoring those scents from afar, it is unwise to get too intimate with your soil when it's thawing. Resist the urge to finger it. Yes, you can go out and dig in eventually. But you should really wait. Fiddling with the earth too early turns it into a mucky mess and forms major fault lines. I have tried to sow too early and suffered the consequences of the overly ambitious. Except for a thin row of peas plugged in with minimal interaction, I wait for warmer times. Instead, why not take this moment to perceive your garden? Get to know it through your nose. Exercise a sense that you sometimes don't plug in. And enjoy it purely on a sensory level. Part of the ecstasy of the first sniff of spring is that it requires no work whatsoever. No need to feel guilty. Yet.

BURY YOUR NOSE

S PRING IS SUCH a wake-up call for your nostrils. Sure, winter has its perks for a nose, but a keen sense of smell was more of a liability and less of a benefit when the garden was slumbering. Mothballs, stale woodsmoke, kitty litter, and the like were the stimuli that tended to entertain your nose in the cold months until the ground thawed. And then good things start to happen. Thank goodness violets are some of the first flowers to blossom in spring.

If you don't know why I'm mentioning violets and fragrance in the same breath, join the crowd. Although you might purchase a plant in the *Viola odorata* contingent like 'Freckles', your nose is apt to be disappointed. Unless you find the rare 'Rosina', smelling a violet is going to leave your nose unfulfilled. That wasn't always the case. At one time,

The scent of *Viola odorata* var. *rosea* is so high-pitched that it can exhaust your nose.

violets were clutched as nosegays meant to distract the sense of smell during too-close-for-comfort social situations when the body odors of closely congregated, nervous human beings might become a little too effusive. Nosegays were de rigueur for the theater-going crowd, and violets were an effective diversion tactic. Extremely high-pitched, with a sugary candied scent that is coyly fleeting, there is nothing quite like a violet's aroma. Light and ethereal, it floats away. In fact, not everyone can perceive it. But for those of us who can, it's addictive.

Young ladies were once taught how to sample a violet's wares. They were instructed to take dainty little whiffs of their nosegays rather than indulging in one vulgar inhalation. From a nostril's point of view, that makes perfect sense. When you breathe deeply, a high-pitched scent can elude your olfactory bulb. Dainty whiffs send the scent to the right place. And a violet has a very unique scent. Although totally divine, it has the ability to block your nose from perceiving its high-pitched aroma for the next twenty minutes or so. Only wallflowers share that trait.

The flowers of *Viola odorata* and *V. odorata* var. *rosea* are tiny, which was ultimately one reason for their undoing. They did, however, enchant Empress Josephine, who cultivated those ultra-fragrant blossoms at Malmaison. 'Marie Louise' (named for Josephine's nemesis and the second wife of Napoleon Bonaparte), 'Lady Hume Campbell', 'Duchesse de Parme', and 'Swanley White' were wildly popular in the second half of the nineteenth century. But with time, breeders began selecting for larger flowers, longer stems, and chubbier blossoms for bunching purposes in handheld bouquets. That's when the fragrance went south. Nowadays, it's nearly impossible to find a fragrant violet. However, if you can locate a patch, get down on your knees in earliest spring and sample a flower. It's memorable. The single-flowering varieties tend to be ultra-hardy; the distinctive double types, unfortunately, are tender and best grown in greenhouses.

It's difficult to find truly fragrant wallflowers. Like ten-week stocks (which are another ultra-sweet perk of spring), they burst into blossom quickly and fade almost as fast, especially when the weather is warm. Originally known as *Cheiranthus cheiri*, they have been reclassified as *Erysimum cheiri*. Each flower is small, but they bundle together on the stem to form a more impressive show. In cool weather, you might get a couple of weeks of sugarcoated, clove-scented pleasure from the clusters of blossoms, but they tend to stop blooming when toasty swimming weather hits. Neon-colored 'Orange Bedder' is the only representative I can find on the market. But 'Bowles's Mauve' (if you can get it) is so much easier on the eye. If only I could obtain 'Apricot Twist', which is a wallflower-blooming cranberry with orange streaks, I'd be in seventh heaven.

If you like fleeting, ultra-aromatic spring performers, try mignonette. Not only are the flowers of *Reseda odorata* spicy, but they also have a seductive vanilla undertone that is the stuff of dreams. Unfortunately, they like cool weather, wilt in the heat, run up to blossom in a few days, and go to seed. And their virtues are limited to the aromatic arena. There's really nothing much to see. The flowers look like a diamond setting, but without the diamond. And the analogy is also apt for the size range: little. It's totally about the fragrance.

Violets, wallflowers, and mignonette are great fleeting spring flings, but give me clove pinks any day. Dianthus flowers are in it for the long haul. Not only are they associated with spring, but the pageant also persists into summer. And that scent! Cloves and cinnamon. During the day, you need to take your nose directly to the flowers to perceive it. In the evening, the aroma floats lightly on the air like distant cinnamon buns. Mouthwatering. And the colors! From the seventeenth century onward, gillyflowers were bred with bands, streaks, and dapplings of vibrant colors. Some have frilly petals, while others are double. They are all delightful to behold. Compared to the other blossoms mentioned here, dianthus are the overachievers size-wise, usually about an inch or so in diameter. They are not huge, but you can definitely see them from a distance. However, not all dianthus are fragrant. The so-called cheddar pinks (*Dianthus gratianopolitanus*), such as 'Firewitch', 'Tiny Rubies', and 'Pike's Pink' (to name the most common), lack aroma. Likewise, carnations (*D. caryophyllus*) were bred for long stems and tend to disappoint your nose (the gene for fragrance is not linked with the characteristic of a long stem). Buy dianthus in flower at the nursery and test its smell firsthand. Not a bad way to spend a spring shopping spree.

DAFFODILS

W E EXPECT PERFUME to float from cinnamon pinks and the like, but spring holds some surprises. Fragrance might not be what you first associate with daffodils, but it's time to expand your horizons. Sink your nose into some of those trumpets. Everyone talks about the somniferous effect of the poppy fields. Well, the sultry perfume emanating from an ocean of naturalized daffodils at a certain time of day makes me equally lethargic. Wade through daffodils on a warm, sunny spring day around high noon and you might not swoon, but your eyelids are apt to grow heavy. Naturalized fields of daffodils always say siesta to me.

We all know about the radiance of daffodil colors. The earliest daffodils tend to wear strident firefighter yellow. It's like someone designed daffodils specifically for shock appeal. You can't miss that color, and that's just what you want when it comes to pushing winter aside and moving on. But what about the aroma? Even the catalogs just give it a polite nod. I say it's high time to appreciate narcissus for their full repertoire of talents.

To describe daffodils simply as fragrant is like saying chocolate is sweet. There is so much more to the sensation. Every daffodil has nuances of scent, and the harmonies change at different hours. My jonquils say very little in the morning. By noon they start talking to me. At dusk they speak loud and clear of warm powdery doughnuts. But not all narcissus follow that pattern. Some are stronger at noon, like 'Pimpernel' (yellow petals, orange cup), which sends out the essence of vanilla custard just when your tummy is rumbling for lunch. 'Kedron' (creamy yellow petals, orange cup) emits a totally plausible imitation of eau de suntan lotion. 'Cheerfulness' (creamy white double with yellow flecks) is Ivory soap. 'Marieke' (school-bus yellow) is candy cane dusted with vanilla. 'Mount Hood' (all white) is rose face cream. But 'Thalia' (also white) is the aromatic equivalent of gym socks. And that's just the quick tour.

Many jonquils are hardy enough to tolerate New England winters but are also okay with the lack of cold weather in the South, and their fragrance is intense.

The intensity of their fragrance is affected by whether you grow your daffodils in full sun or partial shade. The soil in which your daffodils are anchored can also make a difference. Even the temperatures can affect how much aroma each flower pumps out. Those inputs often sway scent and its profusion. Just like we are what we eat, flowers are the sum total of their incoming data. So visit lots of daffodils at all times of day, and be inquisitive. Get up close and personal with a narcissus. However, be warned: daffodils are not edible. No matter how much they smell like macaroons, do not nibble. They are poisonous, which is one reason deer spare their lives. But they can prompt you to make a detour to the bake shop on the way home from Easter festivities, or totally ruin your Passover resolve.

As for the fields of naturalized daffodils, they are usually composed of a combination of the hardest-hitting, strongest, most disease-resistant multipliers in the narcissus kingdom. We're talking 'Mount Hood', 'Ice Follies', 'Marieke', 'Salome', 'Cheerfulness', and similar survivors. Their flowers have good substance and have been bred to withstand the elements at a time of year that can be dicey. In addition, many are intensely fragrant. Put them all together, wade through a few hundred thousand flowers, and you are going to have an intoxicating experience. But that's what spring is all about, right?

TARTS OF SPRING

D ON'T GET ME started, but doesn't it sometimes seem as though the industry is eye-driven rather than catering to some of our underused senses? Noses deserve equal time. Not all of spring's scents are subtle. At other times of year, the word *tart* might seem like a criticism when describing a flower's aromatic offerings. Indeed, coupling a flower's attributes with anything associated with a bar scene might not be viewed as desirable. But we cut early spring a lot of slack. When Korean spice,

Viburnum carlesii, opens its plump cymes of pink-tinged blossoms at the crack of spring's first rustlings, we gush in sheer ecstasy and apply our nose repeatedly. The fact that the overblown combination of vanilla, baby powder, and spice has a hint of bodacious locker room beneath all its good stuff doesn't faze us. We are just glad for an excuse to touch our nose to something other than an icicle.

The scent of *Viburnum carlesii* is a life raft. It is pretty much the first shrub to perform in spring (if you discount the witch hazels, which are more aptly classified as winter fare), and we clutch onto those flowers for dear life. Nothing smells as welcome as Korean spice. It begins blush pink, ripens to ivory, and unfurls on naked stems—and we cherish every whiff. But in truth, would you love that brazen aroma in another season? Perfumers would likely label the scent as animal. Korean spice is the essence of come hither.

In New England, you'll find Korean spice planted beside old tumbledown farmhouses, tucked right next to the foundation. A fairly recent introduction, the shrub arrived in the early twentieth century and was embraced as a totally bulletproof precocious spring performer with a slightly naughty scent. Its popularity probably lay in the fact that the hyper-early flowers are a symbol of hope, just like crocus. Or you could read that je-ne-sais-quoi undertone lurking beneath each inhalation as one of the rites of spring, with its bawdy pheromones and wink-wink proclivities that even the meanest hard-nosed Yankee couldn't resist. If you were to distill the quickening of your heartbeat and the temperature rising in your libido into a blossom, it would be a Korean spice flower.

Following close on the Korean spice's heels is *Viburnum ×juddii*, with a similar scent minus the slightly rank undertone. In just a few weeks' time, other fragrant viburnums will fill out the aromatic spectrum. From *V. ×burkwoodii* (I haven't sampled it, but Michael Dirr labels it as daphne-scented), to *V. ×rhytidophylloides* (I'm going to call it the combined forces of vanilla, baby powder, and cinnamon), many viburnums put spring on the map for your nostrils. As for *V. lantana* (wayfaring tree viburnum), its scent is not heavy, but if you apply your nose, you will be punished with eau de body odor. I detect no scent at all wafting from the doublefile viburnum, *V. plicatum* f. *tomentosum*, and its progeny or from *V. sargentii*, although both are spring-blooming shrubs worth growing

from a visual standpoint. When it comes to spring's framework, they create the critical mass. Later, *V. dilatatum* selections open; one is 'Henneke' (Cardinal Candy), which has an unabashedly musky top note. I love that scent, but just to put that in perspective, I don't find skunks offensive from a distance.

If I could grow daphnes, they might challenge the Korean spice to a race for first place in the spring lineup. Maybe it's my soil pH (daphnes prefer acidic), maybe it's some other quirk of my property (such as the poorly drained soil), but they don't like my land. Fortunately, I get the

Viburnum carlesii isn't called Korean spice for nothing.

vicarious olfactory experience. I visit enough gardens where it thrives to know that the fragrance of *Daphne ×burkwoodii* 'Carol Mackie' is thick, musky, and totally unique. The perfume of daphne is legendary. I'm not sure about pollinators, but grow it, and I will come.

Winter honeysuckle, *Lonicera fragrantissima*, is not as readily grown as the mainstays previously mentioned, but it deserves a greater following for its aroma and the service it performs in occupying early-flying bees. It possesses a high-pitched scent that plays counterpoint to many of the other deep-throated aromas of the early season. I've never actually grown this shrub with its tiny pearly white flowers in clusters. But I sampled it when the crocuses were blooming at the New York Botanical Garden, and the event was memorable. At midday, it kept its aroma close. At other times of day, that might not be the case.

I've always wanted an abelia, so when Broken Arrow Nursery brought a handsome shrub of *Abelia mosanensis* to a show, I followed my nose to the small bush. While burying my smelling agent in the plentiful pink-white flowers, I caught sight of a tag with a zone 5 label (rather than the zone 6 usually associated with abelias). Needless to say, it came home with me. The spring fragrance is similar to the full-bodied aroma of Korean spice, but spares us any of the negative undertones and adds a hint of tea rose to the brew. It is knock-'em-dead delectable, and the nursery promised me raging autumn color as well.

Not everyone associates aroma with mock orange, *Philadelphus* hybrids. In many cases, breeders labored so hard to improve the blossoms that they lost the scent in the process. If you can find a good old-fashioned single-flowered *P. coronarius* and apply your nose to its late May and June blossoms, you will smell the sugarcoated citrus that earned this plant its common name. Although the growth habit might be awkward compared to the tight little buns of the hybrids currently on the market, it's worth seeking out the original species for the fragrance.

LILACS

Y OU DON'T HAVE to go looking for lilacs. They grope for you in the dark, sending their seduction into your nasal passages. They float on the air, spreading their signature musk hither and yon. Eau de lilac is especially thick after a spring shower, maybe because the air is dense and sticky with scent. And there is no aroma like a lilac. It is a sensation unto itself. Nothing matches it; nothing can compare; there is no analogy. It changes with the weather and the time of day, but it's always there— sometimes faint, sometimes heady.

In May, I could do my evening walk blindfolded. I might come home with multiple fractures, but I would know where I was in the neighborhood. That's the senior center on my left, with a grove of lilacs by its door. I'm almost home judging by my neighbor's *Syringa vulgaris* 'President Lincoln' throwing its scent across the street. If a breeze comes up (and May tends to be big in the breezy department), the scent might become diluted. But my nose would still detect the diffuse hint of lilac and know that my neighbor's glistening white flower clusters were somewhere in the near vicinity. Everyone plunks their lilacs proudly beside the road in our town, which helps me navigate without a flashlight at night. I'm not sure if roadside planting is a New England tradition, but it's certainly a local practice. I inserted my lilac by the window of my office to let the waves of perfume float indoors. It's one good reason to keep the window open as long as possible in the evening. I put on extra sweaters for my nostrils' sake.

Lilacs are fickle. Is it my imagination, or are they more fragrant after dark? Certainly, their scent is more apt to float around in the evening. During the day, you might have to apply your nose to the flowers. After dark, it's a different story. As far as I can decipher, although lilacs do attract pollinators, night-flying insects are not their main target. The atmospheric conditions must be the deciding factor, or it might be a breeding phenomenon. I have a friend with a lilac collection beating a path alongside the ocean in Maine. A fisherman once told her that even in fog (maybe especially in fog), he can smell her lilacs out at sea.

How to describe the scent? It's thick, seductive, intoxicating, heady, and universally adored. It's the stuff of cardiac flutterings. Close your eyes and you can conjure it up. Do you smell it? Anyone who dislikes the scent of lilac would be a curmudgeon to a degree beyond fathoming. Some lilacs are more heavily scented than others, but most possess a scent of baby powder and vanilla heavily laced with wine. Perhaps a touch of cinnamon tossed in. Perfumers find a hint of honey in the makeup of *Syringa vulgaris* and maybe a jasmine undertone, but these are only nebulous correlations. Of course, not all lilacs are created equal. White lilacs tend to be the most fragrant. *Syringa vulgaris* 'President Lincoln', 'Rochester',

---

The intoxicatingly thick scent of lilacs floating on the evening air is the stuff of dreams.

'Charles Joly', and 'Flower City' are all intensely aromatic, while the bicolored flowers of 'Sensation' strike me as being slightly wanting in the scent department. Some aficionados observe that the older hybrids are more endowed with perfume compared to newer cultivars. This could have something to do with larger florets in the human-enhanced spires substituting size for scent.

If you wanted to indulge in lilac ecstasy for as long as possible, start the floral festivities early and try *Syringa ×hyacinthiflora* cultivars such as 'Pocahontas'. To extend the sensual lilac experience beyond the May burst of bloom, go for the Japanese tree lilac, *S. reticulata*, which reaches tree proportions and produces white-blooming panicles in midsummer. Less fragrant by a long shot are *S. meyeri* and its progeny, such as 'Palibin', with a fragrance optimistically described as faint.

For all their fragrant virtues and visual appeal when in flower, lilacs are not a wonderful experience for your eyes after blossoming. You can counteract their gangly growth habit by snipping bouquets of blossoms for Mother's Day. This shrub pleads for pruning. Stronger measures will be needed as it grows older—eliminating old, woody growth is the only way to keep a lilac presentable. 'Prairie Petite', a new *Syringa vulgaris* selection, forms a tidy, rounded orb, and it possesses a delightful and rich scent.

Also on the detriment list for lilacs is the powdery mildew issue. Great air circulation is the best preventive measure. Although unsightly, the mildew does no permanent damage to the longevity of the bush. So lilacs are gloriously imperfect shrubs that we love despite their flaws. You just have to enjoy them on their own terms. And I'll be the first to testify that you can forgive all their other imperfections on a May evening when dusk has descended and your nose is in desperate need of a little happy hour.

Sound

JEEPERS PEEPERS

I'M NEW TO hearing. Until a couple of years ago, when technology gave us better hearing aids, I had never experienced the white-throated sparrow's high-pitched "hey sweetie" pickup line. It was just totally out of my limited hearing range. Once I heard it, I was singing that tune night and day. (I'd like to think a lot of white-throated sparrows were fooled, but somehow I doubt it.)

One spring sound that never escaped my hearing is the peepers. In earliest spring (actually, before spring is official), I go on my daily evening walk—the same one that brings the lilacs to my nose's notice—and head straight for the swamp with hope in my heart. Fulfillment starts with one or two tentative peepers who will undoubtedly be silenced later in the week when the nighttime temperatures plummet. But they have managed to sow the seed of hope. From the first peeper onward, it's officially spring. I don't care what it says on the calendar. I don't care what the groundhog predicted (who in their right mind trusts a groundhog for anything having to do with a garden?). The first haunting crooning of the peepers is the clincher. There's no going back—psychologically, anyway.

It starts with a slight jingle, like sleigh bells. The peeper chorus always echoes hauntingly and it is hard to pinpoint. It dies out entirely for a few chilly evenings. Then it starts up again with a little more fervor as though the tiny creatures are determined to make spring happen solely by their vocalizations. It's like the animal kingdom's version of clapping for Tinkerbell. They will bring spring.

There is a crescendo. They go slightly overboard. The whole peeper chorus combined with all the amorous frogs becomes a din. You can't help but hear it. It's almost deafening. But it's one of the perks of living beside a wetland. The peepers are a good argument for preserving bog ecosystems in all their soggy splendor. For a few unfortunately silent springs, the peepers were muted. Neighbors came up to me at the market with worried looks, asking if it was the end of the world. I didn't have an answer. But the peepers came back again, and hope was restored.

Eventually, my evening walks are serenaded by a full chorus. Now that I have the ability to hear every crooning, I'm all ears. I take tremendous delight in trying to dissect evening noises. I can now distinguish the American robin's squeaky-wheel song from the black-capped chickadee's plaintive note and the northern cardinal's warbling. Behind all that evening song, there is the perpetual jingling of the peepers. Gradually, as I walk, the bird chorus quiets down. Birds tuck in early at dusk, and the American robins are one of the last to call it a night. Finally, the peepers

The first birds of the season are always a thrill.

alone are keeping the night watch (or engaging in whatever peepers do after dark).

Not everyone loves peepers. In particular, people who are new to the country setting sometimes take offense. Maybe developing an appreciation for their jingle comes with exposure. Even if you never get acclimated, the sound becomes less insistent and more like sleigh bells in the distance as the season progresses. But for me, it always has a wonderful lusty quality. Somewhere in the gathering night, all the Jacks are finding their Jills—or at least they're out there trying. The sound of that romance, and its inevitable results, is the essence of spring. For a gardener, it's like the sound of the shotgun opening the race. From the peepers onward, we're off and running.

SUCH A TWEET

T HE FINCHES ARE at it again. What started as some noncommittal rustling escalated into a whole lot of flittering, fussing, and discussion. It's renovation time for the nest. So far, Mr. House Finch seems to be doing most of the heavy lifting. Things are never exactly the way they left them, but they still come back to Home Sweet Home. Several years ago, Finch and the missus found the real estate of their dreams on my front porch. When I hung the blueberry twig wreath on the knocker of an unused door, I figured it would delight the drive-by traffic for the winter and then we would move on to other things. But fairly early the following season, before I had the opportunity to do spring cleaning outside, the Finches flew into town and set up housekeeping in its awaiting twigs. They went to work on the first set of offspring, they were inspired to parent another

---

As far as Mrs. House Finch can figure, the blueberry wreath was hung for her.

brood and then another, and now the wreath is a permanent fixture. It can't be budged, but Einstein and I couldn't be happier.

Before you have a bird, let me assure you that Einstein is solely an indoor kitty. The Finches' arrival every spring is greeted by a whole lot of jumping back and forth between desks and pawing at windowpanes from the inside as he jostles to get a better view, but any notions of finchocide are purely wishful thinking on his part. The Finches seem to know that their nest is observation material only, and they carry on without giving Einstein a second thought—until fledgling time arrives. Then they proudly play to the audience, with general mayhem and vocalizations. They make sure nobody misses the maiden flight of their progeny.

The house finch family is not the first to arrive in spring, but they are my closest neighbors. Meanwhile, plenty is happening farther afield. The red-winged blackbird announces a defiant "tweedle tweedly dee" as he stakes his claim in the cattails. Hearing that song again in earliest spring is my reward for trudging up the hill toward the reed-lined wetlands on my daily walk. What starts as an initial triumphant territorial proclamation by the first red-winged blackbird back in town turns into a raucous fight between red-winged neighbors vying for the best nesting site, the cutest girl, or both. When the early March winds are howling, there is a combined ensemble. The grasses sway, the blackbirds do death-defying stunts, and they try to get a boastful song in wherever possible.

Every day, more arrivals add to the symphonic sound. Pretty soon, the air is joyous with the general clatter of feathered fly-ins. Just a week or two into spring, and we have an orchestra composed of every type of chirp, trill, and twitter imaginable. That serenade is particularly sweet when it's new to our ears in spring. As gardeners, we look over to the magnolia or dogwood and feel the pride that comes when a little foresight furnishes a perch for some weary traveler. If we have planted something truly thoughtful, it just might rate as a habitat to nurture future generations.

As for the Finches, their conversations seem to be limited to a series of emphatic chirps rather than sequential singing. Plenty of dialogue occurs, especially upon first arrival, but it sure isn't music to the ears. Then they become involved with home improvement, which takes all their collective energy. He brings building material, and she fusses around with the actual construction. Every once in a while, Einstein and I hear scratching on the door as nesting ingredients are firmed into place. When construction is finished, things quiet down while the brood is kept warm and cozy. If I come too close for the next two weeks, I get the hairy eyeball. Encroaching on their territory sparks a more aggressive response when the eggs hatch. But birth announcements are eventually sent out. He flits around in nearby trees, serving as a general support team, and serenades his wife with his continual, "Way to go. Good job, babe." When the finchlets are fledging, Mom and Dad have a few panic attacks when I forget to keep a respectful distance. That goes on for a while, and then it's time for the second brood. Apparently, finches are not keen on being empty nesters.

I always wonder what happens to all the generations of finches that begin their life on my door. Do they marry local girls? Where do they set up housekeeping? I never know for sure. But deep inside, I harbor fond hopes that perhaps someone else in town has left a wreath intact on a door a little too long. It might mean everything to a new couple, just starting up and hoping to feather their nest.

THE RHYTHM SECTION

G ARDENING IS MUSIC. A lot is said and written about water music and the tinkling of fountains in a garden. I could talk about birdsong and insect buzzing until the cows come home. But those harmonies are not the only serenade. When I'm in the garden, there's usually some sort of action involved. The melodies of working and using tools are part of the experience. Perceiving those sounds deepens your interaction with the garden.

I'm not talking about weed whackers, chainsaws, or lawn mowers. I'm referring to the rhythm of wielding hand tools. The thumps and the clicks of your tools add another layer to the gardening experience. Not only do you make music of sorts, but the syncopation can also help you to garden more efficiently and less strenuously. If you establish an even thump, thump, thump when you're hoeing, the rhythm smooths the action. You reduce physical stress and strain, and you save energy—your own energy.

Hoeing isn't the only chore for which establishing an audible routine lightens the workout. I do it with hedge shears, too. I haven't sprung for power tools for shearing; I still clip, clip, clip. The result is more control and less margin of error—or at least that's what I tell myself. And it's so much easier to accomplish the job if you get a rhythm going. You apply the shears to the contours that you're trying to establish, you start working around in an arc, and pretty soon the clippers are almost self-motivated. If nothing else, it's more fun.

By extension, hand pruners also make a very satisfactory clicking noise when they swing into action. Unlike hoeing and hedge shearing, you can't always do this job rhythmically—pruning often requires more than a little thought between swipes. But there is something audibly satisfying about it, almost like music. Not everything needs to be an even beat.

Repotting definitely has the potential for rhythm. In spring, we're all madly transplanting flower and vegetable seedlings from their community seed flats to individual containers before their permanent switch into terra firma. I'm a stickler for wedging soil snugly around all the roots, and I do so by tamping the pot on the bench to help the soil settle in. I once did a demonstration for second-graders and called it the music of potting. Tamp tamp tamp, pause to grab another pot and stuff some potting soil in, tamp tamp tamp again. When you're dealing with hundreds of seedlings, the rhythm makes the whole thing go so much faster. And describing how to pot by ear definitely helped the kids get the hang of it.

Other actions and tools in the garden also have a voice. I don't scythe my field (partly because I want my body left in good working order at the end of the growing season), but I know people who take delight in the sound of that archaic method of cutting grass. Speaking of scything, I should sharpen my tools more often, if only to listen to the blade running over the whetstone. Or you might try to get a beat going when transplanting a flat of newly purchased plugs into a section of soil or edging outdoors. It just brings the whole experience into a different arena. Basically, anytime you accomplish a repetitive task or use a tool, you can make music. But that squeaky wheel on the wheelbarrow is something that you might want to fix.

If you don't get a beat going while hoeing, the work is twice as hard.

Touch

HANDS DOWN

I F IT WEREN'T for the peas, I would keep my fingers out of the soil in spring. Sowing peas is always a painful experience. On the one hand, you wait poised for that moment when the soil is sufficiently thawed to allow you to push some presoaked fattened seeds into its chilly surface. On the other hand, it hurts. Even though I tackle only the actual seed insertion bare-handed, planting presoaked peas invariably leads to soggy gloves while doing the prep work. With temperatures barely above freezing, soggy translates to stiff, tingling fingers, plus you're kneeling on the ground, trying to accomplish intricate work where snow recently melted.

But who doesn't get a little thrill out of this moment? It's the initial opportunity for up-close bonding with the soil. All actions besides the delicate work of planting seeds start with sheepskin-lined winter gloves, but dexterity is not their strong suit. As soon as it's feasible to switch to mud gloves, it's time to trade off hand gear as an official first rite of spring. My preferred spring handwear is latex-coated cotton gloves, which add warmth while providing great leverage. Leverage is an issue because, if possible, you might as well dispense with a few precocious weeds while in the pea-sowing process. You tidy up and ready the plot to receive compost. And it feels ecstatically like honest-to-goodness gardening again. Sure, the ground is still hard, but at least we shook hands.

Aside from planting peas, try to leave the thawing soil alone until mud season is over and the ground is soft and malleable. When it's not thoroughly thawed, the soil forms clumpy clots after you've attempted to work it. Smaller seeds, like lettuce and spinach, get heaved up if they precociously germinate, or they tumble into a crevice. And there's no point in transplanting anything—it's impossible to firm the half-frozen soil around

(FOLLOWING PAGE) The weather is chilly and the soil is cold, but you'll be planting the first peas of spring bare-handed.

the new roots. With just your own hands and a shovel to work with, best to stand back and let the season unfold.

Holding back takes all your powers of restraint; some call it nervous energy (my mother would label it *schpilkis*). It's the itch toward action when you should just bide your time. That is what we're up against in early spring. The sun is just beginning to kiss the earth. We would like to make contact. And it looks so inviting from indoors. The moment the snow disappears, the instant the temperatures shoot above freezing by a few degrees and stay that way for several delicious days, we can hardly refrain from engaging with the soil. That's what peas are for.

HAND SOWN

A FTER THE PEAS are tucked in, the momentum gains pace. Spring just sort of sprouts up. From early March onward, everyone is immersed in the über-focused business of sowing. At Furthermore, seed sowing commences indoors with the ceremonial planting of the leeks. The official starting gate is the potting bench, which is scattered with packets of just about everything from cabbages to columbines. Over the next few weeks, seeds as simple as marigolds and as challenging as delphiniums are tenderly buried in the soil of seed flats. Seed sowing is a ritual to be savored. Packets are studied for their germination suggestions; online searches are launched whenever something unfamiliar like *Berlandiera lyrata* is attempted. This is more than just a chore, it's a celebration. Long before it's possible or feasible to safely play in the earth, we are plunging into the potting soil, making spring happen—one seed at a time.

Wherever and however seed sowing occurs, it is always a sublimely tactile operation. Indoors or outside (as soon as it is feasible to work the soil, the festivities are moved out to planting rows of seeds directly in the earth), you need to do it delicately. Although I'm an outspoken advocate for gardening with gloves, this is one instance where gloves get in the way. If you don't believe me, try sowing columbines. Even bare-handed, you

have to handle those seeds with care (especially when you consider that each one costs a quarter or more). You don't want to waste a single precious seed.

The first flower seeds to be flung outdoors are traditionally the poppies. It's a cold custom. Grains of sand are larger than poppy seeds. Poppies love chilly, damp conditions and they need light to germinate. In other words, they should lie on the soil surface unburied. Tasha Tudor, that beloved children's illustrator and legendary gardener, taught me that on the last snow of the year, you don boots, try to estimate where the garden's boundaries are beneath the snow, and toss the seeds where you want a sea of poppies to swarm. It is an act of faith and trust, which is really what gardening is all about. As the snow melts, the poppies get their required chill and wet conditions until they're delivered to the premoistened soil surface. It works like a charm, but the bare-handed process is brutal.

Seed sowing is one of the only garden chores I accomplish without gloves, even for the larger seeds, such as four o'clocks. Precision is required to aim those little nuggets. In the seed flats, spacing them evenly is key, even though they will be transplanted into individual pots in a few weeks. When direct sowing into the garden, you need to make sure that the carrots, for example, don't form a glob in close proximity, even though you will thin them later. Do not waste seeds by sowing them too thickly. To get the required aim, take off your gloves. And wash your hands between poppies, especially if you don't want to mix 'Lauren's Grape' with 'Lady Bird'.

In early spring, seed sowing can be uncomfortable verging on painful, but it gets better as the weather warms. That's a good thing, because there is a lot of opportunity for intimate contact. The seedlings planted indoors will need transplanting from their mutual seed flat into individual containers with organic potting soil. Teasing them apart requires infinite dexterity, especially when you transplant every single sprout. You tuck each one in, nestle some nourishing soil around it, and wish it the best of luck. That sort of thing must be done hand in hand. It is bonding, and it feels really good.

Bare-handed seed sowing is the only way you can be sure
your wealth is evenly distributed.

LOVE HURTS

I NEVER THOUGHT I'd say it but—thank goodness for the grackle. She joined my cleanup crew. She just took off to an undisclosed nest site bearing a beak full of scavenged yellowed blades of blue oat grass (*Helictotrichon sempervirens* 'Sapphire') that missed the rake when I was tidying up. As a result, I have changed my tune entirely about grackles. They're efficient. They're self-motivated. They show up punctually in early morning. And I could use the help.

Spring cleanup is a scramble. I feel like an octopus with a backache. After the shrubs and trees are pruned back, it's all stoop work. No matter how many Salutations to the Sun (yoga speak for repeated genuflections to no apparent deity) you perform throughout winter, nothing prepares you for spring's calisthenics. If a bird can eliminate just one need to bend over, it has won my eternal gratitude.

And my back isn't the only plaintiff. I try to keep my knees lubricated through yearlong exercise. But it has been a long time since I was a toddler, so I don't have constant opportunities to crawl—except in spring. Weeds are particularly opportunistic in spring. An area of the garden will be spick and span in autumn, and then the snow melts and every nasty thing with a deep, tenacious root will pop up where it's not wanted, requiring drastic and immediate eradication measures (dandelions, this means you). Years ago, I planted ox-eye daisies. Yes, they are pretty. Absolutely, they are low-maintenance, just like the seed packet promised. But I planted a population explosion. They are so plentiful that the most efficient method of approach is crawling between their colonies rather than bobbing up and down. Don't try to eradicate them by bending over— you can never get sufficient leverage to remove the full root system. But these are just a couple of the flowering foes that we all battle on a daily

Don't be so quick to clean up. Your discards might be
nesting materials for someone else.

basis. Patricia Klindienst published a popular book, *The Earth Knows My Name*, about ethnic vegetable gardeners. In my case, the weeds know my name. And my address.

And then there's the raking. Where did all those fallen leaves come from? What was the point of the arduous autumn cleanup if not to dispatch them permanently? Somehow they reappeared. In spring, gardening has the infinite, never-done quality of housework. But you can't just use a long-handled rake to do your bidding because last year's leaves are wedged firmly into the grip of shrub stems. It's hand-rake work now. Get down on your knees.

I have no solution for any of the damage gardening does to your musculoskeletal system. Spring is going to be murder on all your moving parts. However, I do have some advice: take a hot bath at the end of the day. As soon as night falls and you can slip away from all the demands of the garden, do your body a favor. Fill that tub with steamy water and slip in up to your neck. Invite a friend. Soak. It's also one of my solutions for tick issues. Evidently they despise lobster-hot water. But if nothing else, my muscles are the beneficiaries.

Of course, another solution is to get help. And that's where the birds come in. The house finches and chipping sparrows have joined in. Pretty soon, they'll have the ugly debris completely removed. If only I could teach them to weed.

SUPPORT TACTICS

IN NEW ENGLAND, the weather infamously cannot be trusted, and spring is when the climate pulls its most perilous antics. Blame it on climate change, but the temperatures in early spring can shoot up to the

The tender growth of a clematis starts its spring journey up a nicely rusted trellis.

eighties and then plummet a few days later to below freezing. These drastic fluctuations occur with distressing frequency. Of course, some damage cannot be avoided when misguided plants emerge and leaf out too early and are subsequently vanquished by heavy frosts. But sometimes you can take action to prevent calamity.

We aren't the only ones touching our gardens. Plants also make contact with support systems and grope around. For example, vines send up their fresh, tender shoots in spring and begin their journey climbing the support you've provided. Clematis, honeysuckles, roses, and several other trusting vines forge tender spring growth when warm weather strikes (or seemingly arrives). Clematis is particularly quick to trust a warm spell and take the opportunity to send very fragile growth upward. Those delicate sprouts, coupled with the wrong embrace, can spell disaster. A shiny metal support might lead to a very cold reception for spring's young shoots. Clematis are common victims, but other vines are also vulnerable. Although honeysuckle vines are woody and impervious to damage, their fragile new spring leaves have been torched by spring frosts. There's not much you can do about their precocious spirit. But you can limit the damage when the weather doesn't keep its word.

Years ago, I bought some bright, shiny metal tuteurs for the clematis and installed them in the garden. They were heavy-duty, handsome, teepee-shaped versions that looked like they could easily shoulder the weight of an acrobatic vine. Indeed, the weight wasn't an issue. But when the temperatures shot up in early April, the clematis was prompted to make tender spring growth grasping the support. Then the temperatures plummeted. The clematis vines got zapped. The same disaster could also occur in extremely hot weather if the sun beat down on exposed metal. Any time a vine grasps something very hot or very cold, there are bound to be issues.

I'm sadder but wiser now. Instead of exposed metal, I purchase galvanized or powder-coated trellises. Rust can be your ally. Better still, a wooden support is not a bad idea (although wood does not have the life span of metal). It's something to think about when fitting your landscape with supports and gardening in the era of climate change. You don't want your plants' early encounters to be hurtful.

ENTRY-LEVEL MANEUVERS

TRELLISES AREN'T THE only touchy-feely accessories in a garden—gates and gardens are inextricably linked. Gardens must be guarded by fences because of the malevolent creatures hell-bent on pilfering their contents, and fences require gates. When I see a garden with a makeshift gate, I wonder at the patience of its caregivers. How do they have the perseverance to continuously fiddle with a flimsy entry and exit? Gardeners go in and out constantly. Having a graceless gate is like battling a clumsy door in your house. You need easy access.

I visit gardens near and far, and I encounter a lot of gates. Although I'm definitely not an expert on the topic, I have formulated opinions on gate handles. Not only have my own hands experimented with just about every handle known to mankind, but I've also watched more dexterous fingers fumble with them.

First and foremost, get a gate handle designed for garden gates. Bathroom latches might look quaint, but they will not endure the rigors of the outdoors. A streamlined handle makes all the difference. Don't condemn yourself to a lifetime of struggle with a pull-cable handle. We have all watched fellow garden-tour attendees fidget and heard their displeasure. Fumbling with the cord threaded through the fence post is a bear. Finding the cord at dawn or dusk (and especially in the dark) tests your patience. Trying to get in or out while balancing a burden in your hands will drive you insane.

Although hook-and-eye configurations are not quite as perplexing, they can challenge your dexterity, especially when you have a watering can in one hand or are trying to bring in a flat of seedlings. And the hook gets iced over easily in a snowstorm. Thumb latches are similarly doomed to failure. With frost heave and all the other vagaries of a changing terrain, odds are poor that the little latch will fall into the skinny groove. Many old metal gates have spring latches: a long lever fits into a groove, and you pull it in to release the gate from its groove. They aren't the worst alternative, but the spring can get stiff and usually requires two hands to release.

I favor a barrel bolt with an easy-release lever and latch grab that catches seamlessly. Heavy-duty garden gate versions have a latch you can release easily with a gloved hand. If it is installed well, you can swing your gate shut and it grabs automatically. I trust it to catch going into the garden, but I make sure the gate is securely shut when I'm leaving. I swear the rabbits test it every morning, ever hopeful that it's been left ajar.

My goats spend their free time planning escape tactics. An escaped goat is the rapid and complete demise of any type of garden. Destruction

Keeping the goats contained and out of mischief requires a latch they can't work—try as they might.

is their middle name. I've seen them tear leaves off trees that aren't even edible. I love that they're smart and playful, but I hate that they can work any type of handle. A hook-and-eye latch is a cinch for a goat. Give them a day, and they'll have it licked (literally). Instead, I suggest a slide bolt for livestock. My heavy-duty slide bolts have a two-part mechanism that must be lifted up out of a grove and pushed over before the gate will open. And these bolts are installed on the outside of the gate, where the goats can't quite crane their necks to fully work the gizmo (believe me, they try).

If you have never really thought about handles, think again. The gate is your first encounter with a garden. Keep it positive.

THE UNTOUCHABLES

I PRETTY MUCH paw my way through spring. We all spend the season groping our way around, sorting out the good from the bad and the ugly. In the greater scheme of the garden, you either gain control in spring or court bedlam for the rest of the growing season (and beyond). It's a uniquely tactile interlude.

What begins as a few gingerly plucks bobbing for precocious weeds escalates into full-fledged downward dog. By the time May is in full fury, I can no longer take the battle standing up. The prone position gives better leverage to get the job done. Not only is groveling necessary, but I also go into battle armed with weapons. Depending on which vendor you consult, the hand hoe I wield might be called a Ho-Mi EZ-Digger or Korean hand plow. The version currently on the market is forged of steel to form a curved blade tapered to a pointed tip. I use the short-handled edition, which gives me the cutting power to eradicate all but the nastiest weeds, because nobody wants to shake hands with nettles or a multiflora rose.

A lot of opportunistic plants are thorny. Getting a grasp on any type of raspberry is no fun at all. Long ago, I adopted a policy of excluding

members of the genus *Rubus*—no matter how handsome—on the basis of their bite (*R. cockburnianus* is a particularly good-looking Don Juan with teeth). Anything that tends to be energetic and bristly doesn't get any further than the driveway. I refuse to be bloodied by the plants I'm hosting. And many thorny plants send out equally armed runners that force you into combat with potentially painful ramifications. Years ago, someone saddled me with a 'Harison's Yellow' rose with rampant wire-thick runners equipped with razor-sharp prickles, and I will never, ever forgive this gift. It isn't called the pioneer rose for nothing.

You can easily put the kibosh on purchasing any plant with a tendency to shred innocent appendages (although, for obvious reasons, catalogs don't always readily reveal this trait). But keeping painful weeds out of your domain is a much more difficult feat. Although I'm 100 percent in favor of question mark, comma, satyr anglewing, and tortoiseshell butterfly nymphs, I refuse to encourage nettles (*Urtica dioica*) in my cultivated garden even though those butterflies dine on nettles as a host plant. The caterpillars can eat on the verge of the property and in the meadow, where nettles are welcome. Similarly, although I am a staunch advocate for consuming tasty, edible wild plants, especially anything loaded with vitamins and nutritious value (and nettles have a wealth of good things in their leaves), I draw the line at trying to harvest a plant that injects histamines, acetylcholine, and formic acid into my unprotected skin. One resource compares a nettle to a hypodermic needle. Like most people, I get a stinging rash from nettles. Although it lasts only a few minutes, it ruins an hour or so. My mother-in-law, Joy Logee Martin, said that nettles sting only when you brush against the foliage. If you grasp them firmly, they don't cause a problem. "Tender-handed stroke a nettle, and it stings you for your pains; Grasp it like a man of mettle, and it soft as silk remains," she would quote from the writer Aaron Hill (1685–1750). No matter how nutritious nettles are, close encounters always seem to end badly. I do my best to eradicate their encroaching roots (using the aforementioned tools) in early spring before the foliage pops up, and I keep my distance later

Stinging nettles might be laudably nutritious, but they have a nasty bite.

I approach poison ivy with even more trepidation. I don't care if it is a native, and I'm equally unimpressed by the fact that its berries are edible to birds. Because I erupt in volcanic welts following close encounters, it's not welcome in my domain. The battle with poison ivy always calls out shovels, trowels, Korean hand plows, and all manner of other artillery. Never try to eradicate poison ivy with your hands, even gloved hands. Always handle it at arm's length, and then strip down immediately and scrub yourself pink with harsh soap. Even then, I hold my breath for a couple of days and curse at the slightest itch.

Spring is the best time to patrol for all these issues. In the case of poison ivy, even before the bright copper foliage appears, the roots can cause even worse reactions than the leaves or vines. And small seedlings send out runners with alarming speed. Scoop it up with a long-handled tool and dispose of it (try wrapping it in newspaper and inserting it in a bag to be escorted to the garbage can) without making contact. Any of these plants will ruin a perfectly lovely spring day. Don't give them the chance.

ASPARAGUS

ASPARAGUS IS HAVING a big moment on the menu. As soon as the weather warms up, it's time to begin surveillance for asparagus noses breaking the soil surface. Actually, I'm torn between my hunger for the first spears of the season (with just a dash of Parmesan and maybe a spritz of oil) and the knowledge that any precocious asparagus that emerges too early is bound to get bolloxed by the vicissitudes of spring weather. I live in constant fear that a late freeze will hit and the lunch of my dreams will have to start all over again. In the best of all worlds, spring would be a smooth progression from cold to asparagus, skipping the yo-yo sequence. Rarely does this happen.

One year, there was no asparagus. I walked the circular path around my garden, and daily I was disappointed. Finally, I hit the Internet to get the skinny on what plague had devastated the asparagus patch. That's when I learned the cold hard facts of crown rot. It's as bad as it sounds. Fortunately, fusarium-resistant (fusarium being the culprit) asparagus is available. After ordering 'Jersey Knight' roots from Nourse Farms in South Deerfield, Massachusetts, we are now living happily ever after. I hope.

There is no such thing as instant gratification with asparagus. After digging your trench, nestling the roots in, and shoveling the good earth on top, you have to wait a few years before the feast. Meanwhile, the closest substitute I could find for an early-season main course was Swiss chard. Nothing against Swiss chard, but it doesn't compare. And it definitely isn't available equally early in the season.

Asparagus is not an instant crop. In the planting year, you have to let asparagus do its thing unhindered and unharvested. It needs to gather power. The next year, you can harvest for a week, but the stalks tend to be scrawny. By the third year, two weeks of asparagus spears are yours for the

Sweet, flavor-packed, and tender, homegrown asparagus makes store-bought seem like tough cardboard. They aren't uniform, but who needs uniform?

picking, and they are beginning to look and taste like the genuine article. The next year, it's three weeks of scrumptious delight, and so on. After a month and a half of asparagus bingeing, no matter how mature your asparagus happens to be, you must let the spears go, opening to form the ferny foliage, while the stems send their oomph into the roots, gearing up for next year. But by that time, you might be sated and tired of asparagus.

During the asparagus famine, I planted flowers rather than weed the empty space (I figured out the cause of the asparagus issue when it was too late to plant replacement roots during the season). The flower mixture grew on me. Now a bouquet of cosmos, nasturtiums, zinnias, four o'clocks, nicotianas, and anything else I fancy for annuals intertwines with the asparagus foliage. It's a pretty picture and it shoulders out weeds. However, I suggest avoiding dahlias and bulbs that attract voles and tunneling varmints—no point in luring trouble into the vegetable garden. (Yes, there is a fence and buried chicken wire, but the extra protection doesn't render the garden 100 percent rodent-proof.)

So far, so good with 'Jersey Knight'. It's living up to the disease-resistant claims. Meanwhile, I'll never again take the melt-in-your-mouth buttery goodness of asparagus for granted. If you've never tried your own fresh asparagus, take my word—supermarket versions are a poor substitute. I'm settling back into my asparagus bliss, hopefully forevermore.

LETTUCE LUST

OTHER PEOPLE DREAM of martinis and lust after fast cars. Not gardeners. We daydream about the moment we will bite into our first succulent, flavorful nibble of lettuce. We drool in anticipation. We

---

Early homegrown lettuce tastes like butter and melts in your mouth.
Nothing from the supermarket can compare.

flip through seed catalogs to savor enticing descriptions of various types. We balance the relative merits of 'Buttercrunch' versus 'Black Seeded Simpson'. We count the days before our first little seedlings sprout in spring. And the beauty of lettuce is that it doesn't take long to achieve satisfaction. In my garden, self-sown lettuce seedlings that pop up unbidden (but greatly appreciated) are readily apparent when it's time to prepare the beds for that season's sowings. I carefully relocate those little volunteers to a colony of other lettuce seedlings. All the while, I'm salivating.

Of course, lettuce is available in any supermarket. But it's never quite the same. When you bite into fresh, juicy lettuce harvested moments earlier from your own backyard, it melts in your mouth. I can scarcely get to the kitchen without nibbling.

Lettuce is a matter of taste, and there are many options. I veer away from the deeply incised types such as 'Tango' and 'Coastline' in favor of something that doesn't tickle while it's going down. In this, I'm at odds with the chefs who pull together artisanal menus. They just love to garnish their creations with a little frilly leaf of lettuce. (Apparently, boutique lettuce is the new parsley.) The good news is that people actually eat these greens rather than shuffling parsley sprigs to the side.

With substance in mind, I'm a fan of 'Buttercrunch' for my first sowing of lettuce. I don't leave a steady flow of lettuce to chance. In spring, the brave contingent of self-sown lettuces are preserved, transplanted to grow where other lettuces are dwelling. You can get lettuce seeds and plants in the ground fairly early. Most lettuces thrive in the cool weather of spring through early summer. I'm trying 'Optima', which is a butterhead type from Fruition Seeds that forms more of a defined head. I also do 'Red Sails' if I want diversity in my color range. But I don't go crazy worrying about the physical beauty of vegetables because I plan to consume them posthaste.

Here comes my spiel against potager plantings. I think all vegetables are stunning. Unless you have late blight on your tomatoes, your garden is going to look just fine. Skip the fancy footwork with the checkerboard pattern of alternating different-colored lettuces that will be wrecked when you steal a head for lunch. Anything that stands between a vegetable and your salad bowl is not a practical or sustainable idea. Instead, harvest your lettuce regularly, grab those heads when they are ready, and whisk them into your mouth. Don't hesitate to harvest because it might destroy a design.

Famished for field-grown greens, I start the season at Furthermore with lettuce plugs to get salads rolling before the seed-sown rows are ready. This part is critical: harden off seedlings bought at nurseries by acclimating them to the chilly spring temperatures gradually. After they've been exposed to the real world, lettuce is amazingly frost tolerant. Plugs have gone down to 17°F without permanent damage. Granted, they looked a little sad and droopy for a while on those frosty mornings, but they perked right up in a few hours. When in doubt after a deep frost, wash off the ice crystals with a rose nozzle on the watering can before the sun hits the foliage. When your primary fantasy is lip-smacking lettuce, you might resort to that sort of action, whereas normal people just trust luck. And in the end, we probably all have lettuce in our salads before the rest of the world is rolling in their greens.

PECKING ORDER

THE NINEBARK'S DAYS were numbered. I had been giving *Physocarpus opulifolius* 'Coppertina' the evil eye ever since it started coming down with powdery mildew on a regular basis. Cut flower-growing friends advised drastic pruning, explaining that their shrubs were never afflicted thanks to frequent thinning of the branches. The suggestion made sense. Good air circulation is known to be a preventive method for warding off mildew. Constant removal of branches led to a particularly wispy 'Coppertina', but the mildew continued unfazed year after year. Not only was the plant riddled with schmutz, but it had also gained a gawky growth habit. Even worse, the ugly picture is positioned directly outside my office window within easy eyeshot of my desk. The shrub was slated for death row.

Then the chipping sparrows arrived. One mid-April morning, before any leaves had emerged on the ninebark, I heard a din outside my window. No fewer than six chipping sparrows were crowded onto that small shrub, twittering away in sheer delight, pecking away at the powdery, mildew-infested branches. It was standing room only on the 3-foot-tall shrub. They took numbers and waited their turn on the adjacent tiger eye sumac. They worked for ten minutes or more (which is forever for a bird), pecking at the wood, before moving on. And then it was time for the house

Prone to mildew, *Physocarpus opulifolius* 'Dart's Gold' might not look wonderful, but it's a feast for the birds.

finch family to eat lunch. They also grabbed a table at the ninebark diner. In between, the chipmunk took his turn, determined to remain balanced on stems that couldn't quite support his weight. And this circus continued. Before the new leaves truly emerged, birds came regularly, taking advantage of the buffet. Perhaps they were eating insects. But clearly, something served as a meal ticket.

Needless to say, 'Coppertina' is staying. In fact, I just purchased two more physocarpus cultivars. I couldn't find a 'Coppertina' at the nursery, so I went with 'Amber Jubilee' instead. I can only hope it gets powdery mildew. You probably wondered why I am including physocarpus in the taste section. The ninebark is not on our menu. But this isn't only about us. When I really started to plug into my garden with all my faculties on high alert, I began to realize the potential of the space. When you start packing a place with plant life, creatures come. They work the space. They find food where we see nothing more than an eyesore. By being present— listening and observing—you realize the big picture. And it is huge. Sometimes one of your tender sensibilities has to bow to something larger. But to tell you the truth, I no longer see the mildew as ugly. It now looks like some starved critter's meal ticket. And I'm lucky to have front-row seats.

Summer

A road race thunders past my garden
every Saturday in summer. I'm convinced
that none of the contestants really see my
plantings. They are all too wrapped up in
pumping muscles, gathering speed, and
getting to the finish line. That's appropriate,
given that they are racing and not on a
garden tour. But sometimes, especially in
midsummer, gardening takes on the same
urgency. And that's not so appropriate.
There are so many rewards available
beyond just winning the dash.

The garden is in full flush in summer, but it's toned
down colorwise compared to spring.

Summer is a frenzy. Of all the seasons, this is the time when the pulsating, throbbing momentum is so apt to sweep us away in its tide. There is an urgency to summer while all the bugs are swarming, blossoms are unfurling, aromas are wafting, tools are waiting—and you are smack dab in the middle of it all. When stimuli strike from all sides, do you take time to dissect, heed, and relish them? Or do you just drown in response, response, response? If so, what a waste.

Summer has so much to offer. Summer is the dribble of the sweat running into your mouth seasoned with a dash of sunscreen and a pinch of bug repellent. Summer is the kiss of the sun on your cheek when it rises at dawn, heightened to its blazing beat at high noon. Summer is suffused color, dueling dragonflies, fattened tomatoes, juicy berries, and rumbling mowers. More than any other time, summer is the season when the full cast is onstage. Granted, that sensory suffusion can read like a crowd scene. You've got to take a moment—more than a moment—to sink into summer and look around. Sift through the stimuli, meet and greet each delegate at the convention. You have to be present; you have to reap what you've sown.

Summer is so dense, I had to pick and choose my protagonists to include in this section. I couldn't possibly profile every incredible plant that is performing right now. I couldn't be in the meadow interviewing the Joe Pye weed and by the road talking to the echinacea while smelling the cimicifuga happening by the birdbath while weeding and wheelbarrowing and deadheading and munching on the vegetables, all in the limited space of these pages. So I focused on the highlights. I chronicled summer as it hit me. But every summer has its own medley. I hope to set you on the path toward suffusion, where you'll take the long days of summer and follow their path wherever your property leads you. If that's in a million different directions, well, you have a lifetime to accomplish this mission.

Think of it this way: you've masterminded a venue with so much to give and share. You've created a place where other creatures will feast, where summer will blossom with an intensity that could resonate in your retinal memory forever—if you keep your eyes wide open. Summer is the zenith of the fervor we call gardening. All the dialogues of summer are clamoring to engage you, and you need to savor those messages. And nobody deserves to revel in the bounty more than you—the maker, the visionary, the collaborator.

It's a tall order. Running around and standing still simultaneously is a challenge of massive proportions. But you can do it. Because all those plants are depending on you, and because heaven and nature are doing their finest work, you need to give it a standing ovation on every front. Being a gardener in summer isn't just about pulling weeds and wielding pruning shears; it also entails embracing the dividends of all your labor. Go for it!

Sight

SOCIAL BUTTERFLIES

WHEN I WAS really young, adults would bend over and ask, "What do you want to be when you grow up, little girl?" I gave them my heartfelt, honest answer: "I want to be a butterfly."

Who doesn't? For their brief existence (smaller butterflies might last only a week in the flying stage, while larger ones often flit around for a month), butterflies wear great costumes and seemingly have a ball. Butterflies cavorting around the garden seem to devote limited time to the serious business of visiting flowers. Instead, they just fly around, flirting with the opposite sex and checking out the smorgasbord. The only guys who really get down to business are those little cabbage whites—and, frankly, I wish that they weren't so industrious (they decimate my broccoli crop in their caterpillar stage). Butterflies are a delight to see in the garden.

Around here, it's mostly fritillaries, Canadian tiger swallowtails, and black swallowtails floating around, plus the omnipresent cabbage whites. If I were going to have one fodder plant to make everyone happy and draw in as much flying color as possible, it would be a buddleja. Their long bloom period makes loads of butterflies happy: they keep pumping out flowers from midsummer until far beyond the date when the last monarch has departed for Mexico. Recently, I watched a monarch chrysalis crack open and begin its stage as a butterfly. The metamorphosis took two weeks as the black-, yellow-, and white-striped caterpillar was transformed. The emergence encompassed no more than ten minutes as it burst from its bullet-size shell, unfolded its wings, and pumped itself up. A couple of hours slipped by as it fanned its wings and readied for flight. And then it was primed to explore the buddleja at hand. Magic shows and Broadway musicals have nothing on the monarch's dramatic emergence.

My neighbor Toddy Benivegna has always had a beautiful, productive vegetable garden. Last year, she decided to make butterflies her mission, with an emphasis on the endangered monarchs. She hit the books and planted all the recommendations appropriate to our region that she could lay her hands on. The butterflies approved of *Verbena bonariensis*,

Buddleja davidii 'White Profusion' (although any buddleja is bound to be a hit), *Liatris ligulistylis*, and *Tithonia rotundifolia*. She clocked in only two monarchs sightings until August (which was still better than none during the previous year), when suddenly her asclepias was literally crawling with monarch caterpillars. She found fifteen before calling me in the morning. By the end of the next day, twenty-eight caterpillars were scrambling around, munching their little hearts out. They pretty much decimated the asclepias crop, but that was fine with Toddy. She brought them inside (predators are among the major perils that caterpillars face, but any caterpillar that feeds off milkweeds is going to taste bitter to birds), raised them in a little enclosure, and let them loose after they ate their fill, went through a few moltings, transformed into pupae, and emerged as butterflies. We hope they will migrate to Mexico, find a habitat intact, and return next summer to pollinate our flowers and delight our eyes.

This is something everyone can do to change the world for the better. The whole process is easy and fun. Growing butterfly plants is no hardship. Some of the most colorful, buoyant bloomers make excellent butterfly fodder. Take *Asclepias tuberosa,* for example. We're talking a prodigious supply of bright orange and star-shaped blossoms, and asclepias are the larval food of monarchs. The flowers themselves are an eyeful. Mexican sunflower (*Tithonia rotundifolia*) is crowned by radiant orange ray petals surrounding neon yellow disk flowers. It doesn't get any showier than that. Of course, more discreet flowers also fill the job description, like liatris, which has wands composed of deep purple blossoms. As for larval plants, I surrounded my herb garden with rue (*Ruta graveolens*) to ward off deer. Ten black swallowtail caterpillars happily munching on its leaves was an added bonus. Parsley has also proven to be a favorite with black swallowtails, in addition to dill and fennel. (But I confess to getting slightly miffed when they demolish my carrots.) Snapdragons and toadflax appeal to common buckeyes.

Every year I happen upon a white hickory tussock moth caterpillar or two. If a monarch caterpillar seems to be wearing pajamas, the hickory tussock version is clad in a plush white fur coat with black accessories.

A Canadian tiger swallowtail alights on a Joe Pye weed in my meadow.

Do not pet this little guy. It is tempting, but he has nasty venomous barbs like porcupine quills that dislodge from him, stick into you, and cause a dermatological reaction. In general, steer clear of intimate contact with caterpillars for their benefit as well as your own. With a few exceptions (tent caterpillars being one), let them go about their brief evolution on the way to something fluttery and pollination-efficient.

Rachel Carson wrote about a silent spring. We also need to worry that summer might lose its critical workers. The disappearance would be a crying shame for our eyes, but it would also mean a tragedy for the environment. Toddy proved that every individual gardener's efforts can make a difference. You can save the butterflies, and it's not a difficult feat. The eyes of the world are on us.

HOT COLORS

TEMPERATURES ARE SIZZLING. The moment the sun rose, it set the entire garden on fire with its dazzling glare and it has nowhere to go but up in flames. In this light, dull colors simply don't read. Summer goes straight for shock appeal with a gaudy wardrobe that follows suit. The playing field isn't particularly vast for high-summer performers because most plants are in a resting mode between salvos. They don't overextend themselves when the temperatures skyrocket, the soil is baking, and the drinks are being rationed. Many perennials just bide their time.

If you crave blossoms in midsummer, bright rudbeckias (coneflowers), helianthus (sunflowers), heliopsis (ox-eye sunflowers), monardas (beebalm), hemerocallis (daylilies), heleniums, and coreopsis (tickseed) are the prime contenders, and none is known for its subtlety. They are all vivid, colorful characters in a range that could easily be categorized as sunshine shades. In the annual realm, marigolds and zinnias rule the day—and they are nothing if not flamboyant. You can tone them down with astilbes and agastaches, but by sheer stridence, the bright brigade is going to win. Might as well go with the flow.

More so-called tasteful gardeners might say, "School-bus yellow? Not in my garden." Traditionally, the staid set would sometimes allow soft, creamy yellow through the gates, but shocking shades were definitely barred. That attitude began to change with time. I like to think that the general acceptance of high summer's suffused colors has something to do with the current thrust to keep gardens performing beyond the spring and early summer extravaganza. Nowadays, we expect a garden to earn its keep throughout the growing season, so we outfit it accordingly. We think in terms of waves of color rather than typecast a garden as, say, the blue

Although the double dahlias are undeniably jazzy, grow some colorful singles for the butterflies.

garden. Plus, and this is really important, we are doing our part to woo pollinators and serve as good hosts. Keeping a garden action-packed and productive is good hospitality from a pollinator's point of view. If strident colors are necessary to make the initiative happen, most gardeners are willing to roll with the punches.

Although everyone loves the simple, innocent daisy shapes of mid-summer, I like to change it up with some knock-your-socks-off dahlias. The single versions of this composite have the daisy shape and please pollinators, but the double versions make my heart race. I grow both. Who doesn't palpitate for the wonderfully quilled doubles that bristle with petals and form titillating balls of color? But you might also consider the smaller types rather than the dinner plate dahlias—go for more blossoms per plant rather than one immense statement perched on top of a stalk that will come crashing down if it isn't staked. The waterlily types are voluptuous, and the ball and pompon dahlias are a close second. And the color range offers all the nuances of a watercolorist, including just about every hue in the rainbow except maybe true black (although deep burgundy is definitely available) and true blue (although every shade of lavender and purple is fair game). The burgundy dahlias tone down the strident colors of summer, whereas the peach selections serve as segue shades to walk the spectrum gradually up to nearby outspoken hues and create harmony. In other words, you can harness dahlias to do your bidding.

Let summer be as noisy as possible, but also work with and integrate its tendency to shout. Maybe an adept garden is really about blending, or the craft of working with nature and adding our voice to the chorus. Perhaps it's all about rallying your available talent and then setting the stage so everything shines brightly.

ACCIDENTS ON PURPOSE

HERE IS A PLUG for the extemporaneous. I'm begging you: leave space for spontaneity. The poppies are pleading, too, so give them a little leeway where they might pop in. By all means, run a tight ship in your kitchen. Marshal control in the laundry room. Just loosen up in the garden.

Maybe the term "happy accidents" pertains only to gardens, because otherwise mistakes aren't usually such a good thing. Skip training your puppy, and it will jump up on strangers forevermore. Turn a blind eye to your bookkeeping, and April is bound to be hell. But when working with nature, chilling out leads to incredible collaborations. You have to leave openings to let the unexpected happen. Poppies are a sterling example.

Although I dutifully go out in late winter with my packets of poppy seeds to strew on top of the last snow, the best poppies are scattered by last year's poppy heads left in place to do their thing. Nobody tells a poppy where to settle; they are particularly independent and spirited. Given a little patch of unclaimed earth, they will pop up. And the results are stunning. You couldn't possibly have done better yourself. In my poppies' case, it started with a little intervention when my beloved editor James Baggett sent seed from the Chelsea Flower Show. I fed that windfall with several trips to Nova Scotia, where I tied ribbons around the stems of selected color strains, resulting in packets arriving through the mail. But the poppies took it from there, hopscotching around the place in subsequent years. I thin out the seedlings so each individual can meet its potential. Beyond that, I stand back and applaud.

But the poppies are only one example of flowers taking their own initiative to make Furthermore shine. The foxgloves went wild long ago, much to everyone's delight. Again, that began intentionally with some foxglove purchases, but seedlings took the invitation and ran with it into all the right places. Similarly, rose campions (*Lychnis coronaria*), those silver felted-leaf cottage garden denizens, began with a few tentative representatives tucked between evergreens that hadn't yet filled out.

Now I don't know where the garden would be without the screaming magenta-flowering rose campion running around in midsummer. The point is, rather than grooming the garden unmercifully, I let unidentified seedlings sprout to see what they become (of course, I know the identities of several rogues who are bounced out upon sprouting). If something comes up and proves to be a nuisance, I can always dispatch it later. And rather than rushing right in with mulch early in the season, I apply it later, when the columbine seedlings are identifying themselves as such. The results make the garden feel and look natural.

Filled with pollen, poppies are the essence of summer wrapped up in petals.

In the vegetable garden, a few cosmos recur from year to year. The johnny-jump-ups run around like rebels, and I sit back and cheer. Ditto for the ox-eye daisies, although they rapidly rev up into too much of a good thing and require brutal thinning. And I've seen gardens where larkspur, nicotianas, and all manner of other little wonders do likewise to best advantage. The result is a garden with personality.

THE SKY IS THE LIMIT

G IVEN A PATCH of land, I'm probably going to fill it to overflowing with plants. I try not to be gaudy. I go for harmony, balance, rhythm, flow, and textural dialogue. But it will be jammed full. That's why I'm grateful for the sky.

For those of us who know no boundaries, the sky is essential because it leaves a space on which we can't really encroach. We can plant trees, and they will mature in somebody's lifetime to fill vertical space. But there is still a lot of breathing room.

I had a neighbor in another town who planted wall-to-wall annuals in a cacophony of colors. The whole yard was brought into the dialogue, and she threw in nearly every shade indiscriminately. The house was white, so the paint job didn't compete with her grab-bag approach. But the garden was overwhelming. You felt the need for smelling salts just to walk by. We all politely applauded her enthusiasm, which is generally a laudable trait when someone throws her all into creating beauty. Yet we felt no urge to follow suit with similar extravagance. But no matter how we felt, nature inflicted its own parameters on her gusto. She could go only so far; the sky was off-limits. Because she never planted shrubs, plenty of sky was visible. And that made the crazy quilt palatable (sort of).

(FOLLOWING PAGES) Except for a curly larch that exceeded its predicted height by a long shot, the garden leaves outer space alone.

Any garden is best framed by some sky. For those of us with fanatical collecting tendencies, this becomes critical. You need some opportunities to catch your breath in a garden. Pathways and brief expanses of lawn or stonework help to define negative space, but if all else fails, the sky can form a border. Factor it in when you're designing a garden. Think about it when you're pruning up trees and shrubs. Send the eye up there and let it dwell on silhouettes. Reflect the azure breathing space down to your feet with shallow pools, rills, and ponds. The wild blue yonder can be additional real estate, just as valuable as the borrowed landscapes of views and your neighbor's outbuildings.

The negative space concept is key, even if you garden in the city. In fact, the void is essential when too many distractions detract from your carefully planned display. You need some sense of enclosure. Gardeners in the Big Sky part of the country spend years maturing their infrastructure to provide a sense of containment. But don't lose sight of the garden's place in the bigger picture.

The sky has the advantage of putting on a sideshow of its own. We take it for granted, but the heavenly display is an ever-changing, ongoing performance, and we're fortunate to hold ringside seats to the sky and its moods. The best part? The sky is free. And you don't have to water it.

THE WHITES OF THEIR EYES

F ROM THE MOMENT it crests above the tree line, the summer sun is blinding. It rakes over the entire garden, bleaching it out. Nothing compares to the summer sun in brilliance. By ten o'clock in the morning, any weed you've pulled is wilted beyond recognition. The sun's beat is

In the shadows of the shade they love, white foxgloves glow.
In the sun, they would look washed out.

brutal. But its glare also has visual impact. You need to select your garden's wardrobe accordingly.

White flowers are perfect foot soldiers for the shade. Given low light, they pop out and resonate to lend a sense of passage and bring outskirts into the dialogue. Ditto for variegated leaves. But in full sun, white blossoms just bounce the bright summer light right back to your eyes. They fail to read as anything but washed out. Especially beside the seashore or any water frontage, white flowers in a sunny location are completely erased from the visual scene in midsummer. The only exception is in gardens that entertain primarily after dark.

Shiny leaves perform similarly. Have you ever noticed that shiny leaves, no matter how small, serve as tiny mirrors that bounce light around? Photographers battle the phenomenon daily in summer, so we try not to time photo shoots for midday. Foliage, even on trees, reflects light and appears ghostly or anemic. The garden looks like it's on fire, but not in a good way.

My first garden at Furthermore was meant to be a white garden. By midsummer, not only had I discovered white's ghostly trait of disappearing in bright light, but I also realized how many shades of white were available. Any color has many hues, but your eye tends to balance them upon recognition. White can be the exception. Yellow-white, blue-white, and cream-white do not necessarily work well together. Blue-white might look dingy, like a soggy handkerchief, beside glowing yellow-white. White petunias don't necessarily waltz beautifully with the white petals of daisies. And of course you never know how these flowers are going to interrelate until the first petals open. Vendors notoriously have trouble portraying on labels just what shade of white a flower will open—and it changes throughout the day. Juggling whites side by side in a garden is tricky.

Further confounding the issue is the mortality rate. Alba flowers tend to be weaker than the species with color from which they come (the exception is a flower that is naturally a white species, such as a white angel's trumpet). Ditto for leaves that have too much variegation. You have double jeopardy working against you.

Think about positioning and the setting when you're selecting flowers. Rather than going solid white for a garden, you might want to sprinkle in just a few white blossoms among more colorful flowers or dilute them between a generous dose of dark green foliage. I like a strong ratio of greenery between blossoms, compared to new hybrids that pack in flowers as one solid mass (hybrid mums are a good example of saturation coverage). Or try using airy little white flowers, like calamint (*Calamintha nepeta* subsp. *nepeta* and its cultivars). They make the light read like a dappled sheen. Calamint planted below my blueberry bushes appears to be a vaporous glow and delights pollinators. Or you could just skip the issue entirely and go with color.

BEYOND SCARBOROUGH FAIR

O F COURSE, BESIDES taste, herbs appeal to the sense of smell. Without their aromatic essential oils, herbs would lack their most compelling characteristics. Burying your nose in fresh marjoram is a heady affair that nobody but a gardener can really savor. It's our moment of hard-earned exhilaration that no bottled, powdered, preserved, perfumed, or packaged marjoram can equal. For your nose, herbs are a brew laden with slightly exotic, sort of heady, mildly hygienic, strongly restorative associations. Sage reminds you of family feasts. Lavender sends you straight to fresh laundry. Both are pleasant and comforting connections.

But sage, rosemary, basil, marjoram, thyme, and many other herbs have a lesser-known trait that adds a textural element for your eyes. Toward high summer going into the late season, herbs burst into flower. In most cases, they don't exactly halt traffic. But there's a subtle beauty to herb blossoms that feels uniquely deconstructed and adds depth and volume to a garden. They might not be standout prima donnas, but herbs can give a garden cohesion. To my field of vision, they are Scarborough Fair personified, a tousled, earthy, slightly rumpled nod toward a more innocent time. Herbs can capture the feeling of a natural garden, and they offer a little usefulness on the side for more practical gardeners. Show me

a planting of winter savory, knotted marjoram, oregano, hyssop, anise hyssop, and thyme all tumbling together, and my eyes will be delighted while other senses will also follow suit.

Most herbs don't have flashy flowers. Perhaps the edible sage (*Salvia officinalis*), rosemary (*Rosmarinus officinalis*), and anise hyssop (*Agastache foeniculum*) are a few ornamentals with herb affiliations that really stand out when they're in blossom. Other herbs just form wands of tiny blossoms that read only when grouped together en masse. But the beauty of many herbs is that they quickly and willingly expand to form

Yarrow is celebrated for its flowers, but it is one of the few herbs grown for that trait.

the volume needed to create a chorus. Similarly, and probably because herbs haven't been bred for blossoms, they don't have particularly colorful flowers. White and pale pink are the mainstay hues. Again, there are exceptions—hyssop (*Hyssopus officinalis*) has periwinkle blossoms on wands that impress from a distance. But even given its potential, hyssop isn't really arresting unless it has formed a substantial clump. And yarrow (*Achillea* species) has jumped ship from its former herbal associations to be harnessed commercially as an ornamental perennial for its umbels of blossoms in festive yellow and paprika shades. Bright orange calendula is similarly striking for its atypically gaudy wardrobe. You are able to notice just one calendula open in the garden, and a field of calendulas can cause speeding traffic to slow. But these are the standouts. For most herbs, you'll have to wait until they gather numbers. Then they turn your head in a demure, understated sort of way. They feel like the essence of the country.

Go with their laid-back demeanor and let herbs grow lax and clamber all over each other. Combine foliage and flowers. Thyme, oregano, rue (*Ruta graveolens*, which can cause a nasty dermatological reaction like poison ivy), sage (*Salvia officinalis*), feverfew (*Tanacetum parthenium*), and basil (*Ocimum basilicum*) are some of my favorite bedfellows. Of course, if you continually harvest them for culinary purposes (although rue isn't in the edible realm), you will sacrifice flowers. But who can possibly keep up with harvesting herbs when they start spreading around lickety-split? There is plenty for dinner and to indulge your eyes. Eye-popping opportunities abound in the flower garden, so do some discreet dalliances in your edible landscape. Herbs offer so much on so many levels. Let their quiet qualities soothe your eyes.

Smell

A ROSY FUTURE

GARDENING IS A lot about expectations. When you purchase a tomato, you assume it will be scrumptious. When you buy a bench, you look forward to sitting comfortably. And when you plant a rose, you wait for the moment when that first bud begins to unfurl so you can bury your nose in its suffused redolence. If that doesn't happen, you feel cheated. No matter how frilly or floriferous the rose might be, you still expect it to be fragrant. Nostrils that get no satisfaction are understandably embittered.

You have undoubtedly braved innumerable thorns to get intimate with a promising rose and then pulled away frustrated. In the past, many roses were redolent. In particular, roses that were typically grown in gardens entered that realm primarily for their fragrant traits. Then breeders began creating long-stemmed roses for the cut-flower trade, and roses slowly lost their scent. From there, breeders concocted low-maintenance, disease-impervious, ultra-hardy, ever-blooming roses that are probably a godsend—if you don't plug your nose into the equation. But we have associated roses with scent, so anything less seems like an insult.

Every few years, I swear to give up on roses, but then I renege. The moment a rose catalog lands in my mailbox with close-ups of those bewitching flowers, I'm dialing the phone with credit card in hand. But I don't fall for just any rose without carefully reading the description. They might talk about constant flowers, and they might promise painterly colors. But if they don't offer an alluring fragrance description, I'm not impressed. Fragrance is a necessary qualification for roses, so I look to David Austin roses for gratification. The nuances of fragrance in an Austin rose are so multifaceted and complex, they are addictive. Add the wonderful, swirling, multiple-petal forms, plus the spectrum of subtle color variables, and no one can resist. I have been a fan of Austin roses since way back, but when I moved to northwestern Connecticut, the weather squelched that love affair. It didn't seem that fragrant roses and I would ever waltz in this cold pocket of New England. Roses were ultra-expensive

annuals until David Austin offered own-root roses. Then my nostrils' fortune changed.

Most roses are sold as grafts on 'Dr. Huey' rootstock, 'Dr. Huey' being a particularly robust rose with roots that give a shot of strength to get their dependent grafted offshoot going. All goes well in milder climates, and 'Golden Celebration' is its peachy yellow self with a fruity scent. But on a particularly cold year, the rose might die back to the ground, leaving the

Not only are David Austin roses a feast for your nose, but selections like 'Gentle Hermione' also repeat bloom to captivate your sense of smell throughout the growing season.

not-particularly-exciting 'Dr. Huey' to take over with its rangy, ill-kempt growth and semi-double flowers, whereas the 'Golden Celebration' branch is gone. Or, worst-case scenario, the rose might die entirely because 'Dr. Huey' is hardy only to zone 6. That's usually the heartbreaking chain of events. But on the other hand, if a rose is grown on its own roots and bred to be hardy, it might not spring up with a bang, but it gradually survives whatever nature hands out. If it dies back, it grows up again true to name. You get all the goods you bought into.

When the British-based David Austin Roses first began offering own-root roses in the United States, the selection was limited to just a handful of colors. That inventory improved quickly. As of this writing, nearly fifty own-root varieties are available, spanning the red, burgundy, pink, apricot, yellow, and white or cream color spectrum. Many of their most fragrant (and hardy) roses, including 'Scepter'd Isle', 'Lady of Shalott', 'Charlotte', 'Winchester Cathedral', and 'Gertrude Jekyll', are available as own-root options. Disease resistance has also been a strong breeding goal. All these improvements have come to the aid of our senses.

Suddenly, our noses have access to roses, and it changes the course of a day. I come out in the morning, cradle a freshly awakening flower in my hands, and inhale. If possible, I sample several times daily. Michael Marriott of David Austin Roses explained that the subtleties of rose aroma evolve through the course of the day and maturity of the flower. What smells mildly fruity in the morning might wax wildly spicy later on.

Of all the flowers in the world, roses probably have the most diverse assortment of scents. You could wander into the rose garden (if you selected fragrant roses) and witness a medley that includes myrrh, honey, cloves, guava, lemon, raspberry, and tea—to name only a noseful. Years ago, David Austin Roses hired retired perfumer Robert Calkin as its expert nose to translate the fragrances. Who else but a perfumer could key 'Munstead Wood' down specifically into blackberry, blueberry, and damson categories? For the rest of us, it's a daily adventure. Even if you have never tried roses, I invite you to apply your nose and come up with your own heady reactions. Rediscover why roses are the queen of flowers.

RUE THE DAY

I WILL GO to any lengths in the war against deer. There are no limits, no allies I won't rally to the cause. I can't remember exactly how I thought of enlisting rue, but it was probably my own dislike for that herb's acrid scent—it is the polar opposite of the rose perfume. How to describe it? *Ruta graveolens* has such an unpleasantly pungent, vinegary smell that when you disturb its thick blue-green foliage, your saliva wells up. Rue is not edible—indeed, no one is tempted to take a nibble.

From that trait, an idea struck. If we detest the scent, maybe the deer would find it equally offensive. After all, rumor has it that they avoid treading through feverfew, which is similarly rank. So I tried a totally unscientific mini study. A small vegetable garden is huddled behind the house waiting for its fence to be reinstalled after stonework was completed. Brimming with broccoli, cabbage, and similar vegetables, it is designed in a diamond pattern and filled with the sort of stuff deer dote on. An herb garden runs around its periphery for many reasons. Herbs are immensely handsome, and some (but not all) are edible and within easy fetching distance of the kitchen when a pot is boiling and begging for a sprig of oregano. Plus, even the least discerning deer avoid the majority of the herb family. Unfortunately, after a while, deer slowly figured out this diversion tactic. They never ate the herbs, but they figured out that fine dining lay behind the border. That's when I thought of the rue. Although the smell might be annoying, rue is an otherwise handsome spectacle producing a mass of yellow blossoms that stud its sea foam leaves. Maybe it would create a living fence, or at least confuse the issue for midnight pilferers.

The idea was a raging success. Deer, being opportunists, begin to make inroads into the garden. Deer, being klutzy, step on the rue. Deer, being

Herbs ring the upper vegetable garden. Rue serves as the primary player in order to keep deer out.

dumb, assume that the entire garden is filled with this stomach-turning stuff. Unfortunately, bunnies are slightly smarter. And I have discovered that groundhogs also boast an elevated IQ. This plan needs a little perfecting before applying repellents becomes a thing of the past. (I spray the self-seeding prince's feather, *Amaranthus cruentus*, that rings the garden rather than applying something concocted of fermented salmon and rotten eggs on the actual edible plants.) But based on my initial findings, rue definitely has legs as a deterrent.

Just a warning on the rue: it can cause a very nasty dermatological reaction in some people, especially when the weather is sweltering and your pores are wide open and your skin is covered in sweat. Sensitivity varies, and some gardeners suffer a reaction in any weather. Like the deer, I've learned to steer clear of the rue in hot weather. And at every time of year, I arm myself to the hilt when working anywhere near rue, donning gloves and a long-sleeved shirt. Your skin can blister up, and the scars from the rash linger. If you have sensitive skin, this might not be the best deer solution.

But if you love the notion of enrolling plants on your team to thwart the enemy, try interplanting feverfew (*Tanacetum parthenium*) in the herb garden on the strength of its beauty but also because deer reputedly find it repugnant. I've also tried the mole plant (*Euphorbia lathyris*) to protect the sweet potatoes from voles. No dice.

Meanwhile, the rue has allowed another few years of procrastination before rallying a team to reinstall the fence. And in the meantime, it adds a handsome touch intermingled with other herbs. The edibles are planted where I can safely harvest them without brushing against the rue. And the rue intermingles with herbs that aren't harvested for eating, like hyssop and anise hyssop.

Maybe, with your newly attuned senses and your sharpened powers of observation, you will discover ways to use plants that make your world a more productive place. When you get to know nature better, you can form some pretty amazing liaisons with fellow inhabitants of the earth. Sometimes you come to their aid, and sometimes they help you out. Either way, it's win-win.

SWEET PEAS

B Y TWILIGHT, the window boxes that also inhabit the herb-vegetable garden are hidden in the half-lit shadows off the back porch, but the sweet peas sprawling over their sides always make themselves known. I'm hauling buckets from the barn, brushing past groping tendrils on my way to the faucet. And as I bend over to fiddle with the spigot, my nose comes in arousing proximity to one of the floral kingdom's most provocative scents. No other aroma is comparable to sweet peas. The only descriptive analogy might be a warm, freshly opened beehive at high noon when the sun has been heating up the wax and propolis to mingle with the syrupy scent of stored honey. Maybe add a whisper of orange peel. Only after dark does the aroma wander—and not far—but you always know its identity. Nothing else smells like a sweet pea.

But here comes the bad news: most sweet peas no longer smell like sweet peas. When the seed catalogs arrive and you ravenously flip to the pages of sweet peas, tempted by the vast spectrum of hues at your beck and call, keep in mind that fragrance might not be part of the package. Yes, all sorts of seductive shades and combinations of colors can be yours. But they might not all be aromatic. In fact, the fattest flowers on the longest stems with the waviest petals will probably disappoint your nose. It's usually either/or. You can go for the wonderful old-fashioned spicy types with smaller flowers on shorter wands emitting the legendary scent that is the stuff of poetry, or you can make a beeline straight for flouncy. My nose wins every time.

Gardeners have learned to be skeptical about catalog descriptions. When it comes to sweet peas, I trust only the pronouncements of Renee's Garden Seeds and Select Seeds. Somehow, the noses of other seed experts are not always in alignment with my own. When I grow sweet peas, I really want sweet. I don't expect some tiny whiff that will require a whole lot of imagination and wishful thinking. The problem lies in the breeding. Long ago, when florists were striving for those long stems holding beefed-up blooms, hybridizers started working with sweet peas and came back with

incredible flowers, each one sporting glorious wavy edges on wands that stretch a foot or more. But the fragrance was gone. The same tragedy occurred with sweet Williams, violets, carnations, roses, and a handful of other flowers. There were no riots in the street, but some hearts sank. After a generation or so, the public forgot what they no longer perceived. A few catalogs make a point of offering only truly fragrant sweet peas. When Renee's Garden Seeds and Select Seeds say a sweet pea is fragrant, they have sampled the wares and chosen accordingly.

The most fragrant sweet pea I have sampled is 'Cupani's Original'. Stemming closely from the first *Lathyrus odoratus* collected, it is a purple and blue bicolor with relatively small blossoms and only a few per spire. It can't compete with larger brethren, but the scent beats them all by a mile. Beyond 'Cupani's Original', I find that sweet peas in the blue shades tend to be more fulfilling than the other hues from a fragrant point of view. Bicolors in the blues stand the best chance of delivering the goods, whereas bright reds are usually a disappointment.

Siting your sweet peas in partial shade is going to keep the flowers pouring out over the longest window of time, regardless of whether you go for visually jazzy or aromatically sensual. When ordering sweet peas, always look for something that promises heat tolerance. Although I plant them as soon in spring as it is possible to get a window box in gear without chipping away at frozen soil, it's not until nearly midsummer that the flowers finally unfold. They keep on coming heavily and headily, until a heat wave hits. In full sun, this would be the abrupt end to the festivities. In the partial shade by the faucet, they persevere to produce a smattering of flowers until August, when the window boxes are switched into agastache or something more productive. I could economize and do just one planting of agastache in the boxes. But then where would my nose be on the Fourth of July?

'Cupani's Original' and 'Blue Shift' sweet peas breathe out heavenly fragrances that float after dark.

NIGHT MOVES

S UMMER NIGHTS ARE all too brief. I could just wallow indefinitely in the throbbing katydid conversations and the moths beating amorously against the screens throughout those thick, steamy nights. The air is dense, and the temperature has barely budged from its sticky, sweltering daytime high. Climbing the stairs to bed feels like tackling Mount Everest (only hotter). Instead, stay where you are and let the nicotianas lull you to sleep.

Have you ever noticed that night-blooming flowers exhale the most intensely heady scents? Just like many things that happen after dark, their heavy, laden messages verge on impropriety. On the other hand, the midnight ramblers of the flower world are not particularly gaudily dressed. From a moth's perspective (and in our region, moths are most often the target suitors) white or cream colors are easiest to discern after dark. After all, from a pollinator's standpoint (and flowers are all about procreation), how many come-hither vibes does a plant need to lure its eager fans? Flashy colors aren't key when a plant is sending out scent signals. But what really turns on a moth (and I'm projecting here) is musky, fruity, heavy scents. If a flower verges on overpowering and pushes the limits of good taste, it's all well and good for a moth. From our nostrils' perspective, flowers that spew their scents at night might be reminiscent of unsavory after-dark recreation. But that's a value judgment. The brugmansia is just trying to raise a family.

On a hot summer night, there is something mesmerizing about flowering tobacco. No trace of the drama is evident during the day. When the sun is out, nicotiana trumpets spend their time demurely folded—you would never suspect they have an agenda. At dusk, they flare, eventually sending their deep-throated scent floating. You could wade through the redolence, which defines the epitome of a midsummer night. And the

Acidanthera (*Gladiolus murielae*) emits the sticky sweet, slightly musky aroma so in sync with midsummer nights.

scent that wafts from angel's trumpets is several decibels more suffused. Add the sinister element that every part of angel's trumpets is deadly poisonous and the dangling blossoms stretch 8 inches or longer festooning woody mini-trees (related datura flowers stand bolt upright on smaller shrubs, but have similar qualities), and you have the makings of a midsummer murder mystery accompanied by an appropriately disquieting scent. Edward Gorey would approve.

Apparently, moths are hardworking little all-night creatures, given that many flower species lurk only in the dark. Moonflowers (*Ipomoea alba*) are famed for their nocturnal performance. They need steadily warm temperatures, especially during germination, so I've never successfully hosted moonflowers at Furthermore. But I've attended soirées in gardens where the huge white flowers are gaining a foothold on a trellis or arbor. The blossoms look like oversize morning glories, except they do their drama by moonlight. The visual exhibition is a showstopper. However, if you want something with a big, husky voice, moonflowers are not as outgoing as you might hope for a flower associated with femme fatales.

Recently I tried the evening four o'clock (*Mirabilis longiflora* 'Fairy Trumpets'), with its long-throated, glowing white trumpets accented by deep red markings. Their aroma is high-pitched compared to some of the other musky characters on the night beat, but the elongated tube, the fragrance, and the fairy association is enough to get the imagination running overtime. I also tried night phlox, alias "midnight candy" (*Zaluzianskya capensis*), which produced a few shy pink-and-white blossoms that were vaguely similar to phlox in form, although deeply tubular with rickrack petals. I had to apply my nose to the flowers to find their scent, which the Select Seed catalog classified as honey, vanilla, and marzipan. I was thinking along less-poetic cotton-candy lines.

Beside my front door sit a few pots filled with winter-blooming jasmine (*Jasminum polyanthum*), which continued blooming well into summer, grown as filler below acidanthera. Like its fellow glads, acidantheras jut up with tall, iris-like leaves tipped by wands of open-faced flowers. Those broad blossoms are white with red centers and take their turn swelling one at a time. They remain open all day and are also fragrant in the sunshine. But after dark, the scent adds body. It's sweet rather than heady and mixes well with the scent that honeysuckles send forth.

My favorite creature of the night is night-blooming jasmine, *Cestrum nocturnum* (although cestrum isn't actually related to the jasmine clan). It emits absolutely no hint of aroma by day. In fact, the flowers are so shy that you might not notice the night-blooming jasmine is in blossom until evening slips into night. Then *C. nocturnum* opens its very small white flowers and sends out an ultra-sweet scent that is so seductively romantic that it's almost addictive. A coworker at Logee's once complained of insomnia. I sent her home with a night-blooming cestrum, thinking it would entertain her long, slumberless summer nights. A few weeks later, I asked how she liked the perfume. "Never smelled it," she admitted. "I've been sleeping like a baby ever since." Needless to say, the plant became a permanent fixture in her bedroom.

From the porch, the whole conglomeration fits seamlessly with what we expect from midsummer. Mixed with all outdoors, even the headiest night-blooming flower is diluted to just the right romantic proportions. When the evening finally steps into the shadows and I take up my post watching the stars, the night-blooming shift gives moths a preoccupation beyond wooing the porch light. The insects serenade. An occasional possum strolls by. And the night-flowering shift goes to work combined with that faint eau de skunk coming from the undergrowth. It's the stuff of dreams.

SUBMERSION

NIGHTTIME IS AN orchestra in summer, to be sure. But one scent in particular stands out on those sticky, thick August evenings enveloped in humidity so dense that you wade through the twilight. As you sink into a chair and prop up your leaden feet, something particularly dark, syrupy, and molasses-laced floats into your weary senses and lulls you into dreamland. Thanks to the lilies, all the weight and burdens of hot, bothered thoughts turn into something romantic instead. Just when

you thought you could not juggle one more stimulus; just when you figure your senses are sated from the overload that summer doles out, lilies unfold their trumpets. Lilies put their special stamp on the come-hither feel of long, hot summer nights. (Lilies are almost equally effusive during the day, but you might not have as much time to wallow in their offerings.)

For a year or two, I swore off lilies. Between the voles and the lily beetles, lilies were beginning to feel like a seductive summer memory with no place in my future. But who can just leave lilies in their past? With those huge trumpets and the deep-throated scent, lilies are what summer is all about. Just like summer isn't complete without a tomato or two, you need lilies to round out the season. Recently, I buried some lily bulbs gingerly in containers, stationed them on the back porch, and hoped for the best. And because the beauty of containers is you can accomplish planting when you see fit, I timed the deed for late June, when the lily beetles aren't as rampant. I placed them in a convenient spot and watered by hose almost daily while I hit the assemblage of other potted plants. I also monitored frequently for pests. On the porch, nothing sneaks by me.

And that's how I earned blossoms of sticky sweet-scented *Lilium* 'Kushi Maya', with its deep burgundy heart within cream-colored nodding flowers. When it had finished exhaling its last breath, 'Casa Blanca' followed to suffuse twilights with its seductive perfume. Nothing compares to sitting in the dark when the fragrance is diffused throughout the outdoors.

All lilies are not created equal from an aromatic point of view. Stay within the Oriental and trumpet groups if fragrance is the goal, as Asiatic hybrids will disappoint your nose. The Orienpet lilies—hybrids between Chinese trumpet varieties and Oriental lilies—have a refreshingly fruity spin on the deep-throated theme. Some, but not all, of the species lilies feature fragrances. If you want fragrance, check out the description before purchasing lily bulbs.

You might want to keep your lily encounters al fresco. Lilies are extremely toxic to cats. Another issue is that a lily trapped inside is an

The aroma wafting from 'Stargazer' lilies is the intoxicating elixir of summer.

overbearing olfactory experience. One year, the Philadelphia Flower Show greeted the crowds with a garland of Oriental lilies running the entire length of the show entryway. It was overwhelming in a noxious way. What is coquettish outdoors quickly becomes cloying inside. On the other hand, spread over the outdoors, lilies are the essence of summer.

Speaking of deep, musky, overbearing scents, gardenias definitely qualify. Despite the claims of catalogs, gardenias are notoriously finicky houseplants. Instead, think of them as summer fare for the patio. The only practical way to keep this tender plant—which requires several years to reach blooming size—happy during the cold months entails a toasty, humid greenhouse. Given those luxury accommodations, gardenias form buxom, rose-like, velvety-petaled blossoms with an equal outlandish aroma in summer. If you can swing it, they are a boasting point for green thumbs because they require so much fussing and heat to secure those luscious rewards.

Tuberoses are in the same category as lilies and gardenias, with an emphasis on the sensual note. (I've heard them described as carnal, but I wouldn't go that far.) *Polianthes tuberosa* might well make you palpitate. If it goes any further than that (the Victorians accused tuberoses of causing orgasms), you've found better bulbs than I ever met.

Around here, tuberoses planted in spring gear up to the serious business of producing flowers in late summer. Sometimes they open in autumn instead. When they're not blooming, they have long, strappy, ill-kempt leaves. But when the flower spikes do emerge, they form unique creamy buds that open to cactus-like blossoms with pink-tinged edges. Single and double tuberoses are equally aromatic, so you might as well go with the multipetal version. They are infinitely easy bulbs to host, and they tolerate all sorts of abuse. You can also buy them as cut flowers and enjoy all the sensations without any of the fuss. Summer is meant to be seductive, so give it all the ammunition available to make the full swoon happen.

Sound

THE DAILY BUZZ

A T HIGH NOON, my garden sounds like an airport. So many winged things are buzzing around that the only real difference is that I lack air-traffic control. For my midday break, I wander outside to commune with the bugs. Something about hordes of industrious little creatures madly swooping around, coming in for a landing, diving headlong into blossoms, and prolonging that frenzy hour after hour is truly inspirational. (Worker honeybees live only a few weeks, but they are productive weeks.) Watching buzzing things at work will leave you deeply humbled. A few minutes spent wading through a meadow filled with frenetic courtiers milking the clustered mountain mint (*Pycnanthemum muticum*) for all it's worth, and who isn't shamed into hitting the grindstone harder than ever?

I plant for pollinators. It all started with a meadow of beebalm (*Monarda didyma*). From a sensual point of view, it opened my eyes and ears. The beebalm incited my noontime forays into the garden. And the best time to hear the buzz is midday, when the sun too is blaring. Higher temperatures just whip the winged labor force into more fervent efforts. Back then, only a handful of purportedly powdery mildew–resistant bee-balms like 'Jacob Cline' and 'Blue Stocking' were available on the market. Despite claims otherwise, they were riddled with mildew. But the primary problem—and the reason I abandoned the idea of a beebalm meadow—was the fact that monardas tend to be sparse groundcovers and allow weeds to infiltrate. Instead, I merged them into my established meadow, adding the more durable mauve-blooming *M. fistulosa* to the assemblage of meadow plants having a free-for-all in the field. The bee-balms love their new location, as do foraging insects, so I get a noonday serenade. Now I walk through nurseries with an ear cocked for the telltale buzz. If something is humming, I snag it. Innumerable times, I've had to shake off buzzing things before loading. I try not to take bees away from their friends and family.

Reading and heeding suggestions for pollinator-friendly plants has become a way of life at Furthermore. So far, mountain mints (*Pycnanthe-*

mum species) win the pollinator popularity contest, but plenty of close runners-up are in residence. Different species of mountain mint rack up varying consensus numbers. A whole different fan club of bees and wasps pay call to *P. tenuifolium* compared to *P. muticum*, which probably has something to do with the maturity of the flower on that particular day. Different insects have different needs. Watching pollinator parties is like eavesdropping on celebrity bashes with equally outrageous outfits—stand beside *P. muticum* and check out the blue mud dauber's costume. Plenty of plants are on the bee list, but cultivars are extremely variable. Blue agastaches drive flying fans crazy, whereas orange-flowering agastaches have virtually no admirers except a few random sweat bees. Rudbeckias are like chocolate for bees, but related echinaceas aren't equally popular (although butterflies dote on them). And it's not only about perennials. Flowering shrubs can ramp up the numbers while providing masses of food. Hydrangeas such as 'Limelight' draw huge quantities of varied insects and blossom over a long period of time. Mountain sumac (*Rhus copallinum*) blossoms for only a week or so, but during that brief window of time it's like a siren call for a wide variety of pollinators. You can hear the ambient buzz floating in the air from several feet away. It takes all types to pull together a full symphony for your flighty friends. Going for diversity is not a bad plan of action. However, plant plenty of each genus to make the pollinators' work more efficient with fewer trips back and forth.

Once you get into the vibe, planning to keep insects buzzing around is like pulling together a many-course meal. Keeping the food source coming is a challenge and pleasure. A good host doesn't abandon the guests after they've arrived. That's why the berries in my backyard are underplanted with *Calamintha nepeta* subsp. *glandulosa* 'White Cloud'. It's sufficiently airy to allow me to wade in for berry harvesting without ruining the groundcover, a wonderful minty aroma swishes up from the leaves as I move past, the underplanting repels weeds, and smaller pollinators dote on the flowers after they've performed their pollination services for the berries. Plus, the calamintha keeps right on producing blossoms

----

(FOLLOWING PAGES) The meadow is a boon for bees with its lavender-blossoming *Monarda fistulosa*, Joe Pye weeds, goldenrods, and rudbeckias.

until autumn. Then it sets seed, sowing a carpet that becomes increasingly dense. The bees adore it, and so do I.

Dragonflies and damselflies do a whole different zoom. They sound like little sports cars revving their engines as they dart around. They need a nearby body of water (my swampy pond is their ideal) in which to rear a family. Preferably, it should have shelves of soil and upright aquatic plants standing along the edges for egg-laying and resting purposes. And another plus is that dragonflies and damselflies consume quantities of mosquitoes. Meanwhile, these helicopter impersonators are a riot to watch.

Please don't swat humming insects. In general, they won't bother you if you don't pester them. Let pollinators go about their business and they won't be apt to sting, bite, or do you any sort of bodily harm. To help keep them at bay, skip the perfumes when an outdoor outing is planned. Beekeepers also suggest that you avoid eating bananas, which apparently cause honeybees to sting. And, obviously, never go barefoot in the garden. Sooner or later, you're bound to step on a bee and, even if you're treading lightly, it's not going to be a happy encounter for either of you. Watch where you walk, and put in corridors of grass or gravel so you won't be crushing lives. Considering how much effort I put into hosting these fellows (and I'm even gradually converting my lawn to clover as part of the initiative), I don't want to stomp out the good guys. Living in simple peace and harmony gets a whole different beat when the buzz is a welcome sound. Give bees a chance.

TWEETS

I ONCE ASKED Barbara Israel, the legendary high-end garden antiques dealer, "If you could have only one garden ornament, what would you choose?" She didn't need to think twice. "A bench," declared the expert.

Any birdbath will furnish the scene for impromptu pool parties.

"It says welcome." I beg to differ. A bench invites a lot of advice from sedentary onlookers. On the other hand, if you get a birdbath, you can watch spectator sports.

I debated where to discuss the birds of summer in this book. It was a dead heat between Sound and Sight. Granted, there's nothing more wonderful than watching birds frolicking in the shrubs, trees, and plants that you installed specifically for their enjoyment and well-being. Watching birds at a birdbath means witnessing their pleasure as they splash around. But even more wonderful are the sounds birds bring to your landscape, and birdbaths are just one of many lures.

Birds don't catch on to birdbaths immediately. It takes time and a whole lot of surveillance before they discover an opportunity to dive in and drink. I have a birdbath that gets more than its fair share of action. So I installed a second one ("Short lines! No waiting!") within easy view of my office. No takers. And then, one hot summer day, I heard a major commotion. Twittering, chirping, calling, and scolding. Turned out the ruckus was a pool party. Apparently, a horde of feathered partiers was celebrating something, and it lasted just a few minutes while six or eight birds of several different species had a ball. Then they were gone. I would have missed the happy event if the delighted chirps hadn't clued me in.

Siting is critical for a birdbath. There's a half-dead, partially denuded viburnum beside the most popular birdbath watering hole. I left it intact (with some clematis planted at its feet as an eventual cover-up) for the benefit of the bathing lineup. Before they dive in and after they have dunked, birds need a place to perch. The viburnum might not be beautiful, but it serves a critical function. Not only do the birds use it while waiting their turn, but it also serves as a watchtower. The beauty of birdbaths is that they seem to be totally integrated. No matter what a bird's plumage, everyone is pretty much equal at the birdbath. Of course, some of the winged clientele tend to bogart the facility. One sparrow monopolized the water for a dozen dips before he let the rest of the line take its turn. For a while, a crow decided to wash his food in the birdbath, muddying the water (or worse). But in general, the birdbath is both democratic and nondenominational. Of course, there is the potential for party crashers. Stray or outdoor cats could be an issue, so take into account any neighborhood felines before siting a birdbath. At high noon daily, a red-shouldered hawk sails overhead and shrieks. It's nice of him to fore-warn the other birds, which abandon the birdbath instantly. They know when taking a dip is too dangerous.

The birdbath is just one opportunity to heed what the birds have to say. The sounds of summer differ greatly from the feathered vocalizations you hear in spring. Birds switch from amorous expressions to boasting about the brood, encouraging fledglings, scolding intruders, and warning call notes. It's more about chirps, tweets, and calls back and forth than about heartfelt warbling. There are exceptions. Some of the new sounds on the block come from late nesters, like American goldfinches. If ever there was a visible bird, it is the summer plumage of the yellow goldfinch. Goldfinches are also a riot to watch. They are a good argument for letting flowers go to seed rather than deadheading. One of the best things that I did from a goldfinch point of view is plant yellow *Scabiosa columbaria* subsp. *ochroleuca*. Watching goldfinches perform their acrobatics on their wiry stems is one of my favorite midsummer amusements. They also bounce around on *Verbena bonariensis*, agastaches, echinaceas, asters, and Joe Pye weed while carrying milkweed seeds to their nests.

If nothing else, consider planting trees for birds to roost on and vocal-ize. Although the American goldfinch is adapted to the prairie and can sing on the wing, most birds prefer to flit from limb to limb. Once they are comfortably perched, then they begin crooning. I figure that a tree isn't mature until it has cradled its first feathered visitor. If a tree can hold a nest in its boughs, all the better. For that purpose, I leave vines of nonin-vasive honeysuckles (*Lonicera sempervirens* and *L.* ×*heckrottii*) partially unpruned. Birds flit back and forth, jockeying for position and chirping excitedly. Territorial dramas are played out. Family feuds are articulated. But for the birds, the whole place is a major playground.

STORMY WEATHER

I N ALL THE world, few sounds are as soothing as the gentle pitter-patter of raindrops on the earth. Those raindrops merge together, they amass into drips, they might even strengthen (if we're lucky) into a steady tympanic rhythm. Usually, everyone welcomes a few hours of precipitation. When it's constantly cloudy and inclement, or your garden club is marching in a parade, then you might take issue. But a few hours of rain, or even a whole rainy day, is usually good news. You listen for it, you plant seeds with a prayer on your lips for a steady drizzle, you hang out the laundry as a sacrificial offering. Any contribution to ease the constant haul of watering cans is appreciated. However, savage storms are another matter entirely.

Every thunderstorm has its own soundtrack, and the prelude is a hint of the histrionics in store. When you hear rolling and rumbling in the distance for half an hour or more, you're in for a long siege. When the skies are placid and blue one minute and calamitous in the next blink, it's going to be fast and violent. Of course, that theory doesn't always hold sway. But in New England, you can pretty much figure out the severity of what's coming by the preamble. It often (but not always) forecasts the difference between a few snap, crackle, and pops compared to piercing, stabbing, ear-splitting, and potentially deadly firebolts from the sky combined with pummeling, gully-washing rivers of rain. Listening for weather warnings also helps. Whether you relish the forecast has a lot to do with where you are, how much your garden needs rain, and whether you have a tour scheduled for that afternoon.

I'm deathly afraid of thunderstorms. I'm scared of the rolling thunder kind and I'm petrified of the lusty, punishing, crashing versions. Many years ago, a horrific flash of lightning hit the goat barn, killing one of my favorite Saanens, and I never truly recovered. Although I realize that summertime thunderstorms are a natural fixture of New England, they stop my heart. I have installed lightning rods on the house and I always seek shelter, but I still put on my rubber boots although safely indoors. When I'm on the road, I monitor weather forecasts obsessively when stormy

weather is predicted. Not only do I seek cover starting with the first distant flash, but during a thunderstorm you won't catch me sheltered in a building that isn't at least 100 years old.

However, there comes a time during every prolonged drought when I'm willing to take precipitation in any form. With everyone else, I watch helpless as it goes gushing down driveways (mine is gravel) to find someplace to gather together. On my property, the rivulets cut right through the middle of the birdbath garden, taking all the mulch with it. From there, they head down to dislodge the bulbs planted beneath the black walnut. In a prolonged deluge, the water will make its way through the meadow

Raindrops roll off the hosta leaves.

to the vegetable garden and redistribute the pebble mulch before settling into the rain garden, hopefully before hitting the pond.

I don't have a real rain garden. It's just a low-lying pocket holding lots of particularly thirsty plants. Somehow, it seems to work. I installed it before the rain garden fad, so it lacks the layers of drainage stone underneath that define a true rain garden. But those thirsty plants—like every mountain mint (*Pycnanthemum* species) that I can lay hands on, as well as heliopsis, physostegia, and helenium—do a fairly efficient job of slurping up stormwater before it reaches the pond. The only problem is that weed seeds also follow the water's course, coming to rest in the rain garden and ultimately sprouting and wreaking havoc. As a result, the rain garden requires two-fisted patrolling for weeds and invasive plants. Every unsavory green character in town is going to lodge itself in that garden sooner or later, but maybe other bad stuff won't make it into Lake Lauriat, which is what they call the tiny pond at the end of my property corridor. It's worth a little weeding for the greater good.

You can learn a lot from thunderstorms. Not only are they terrifying, but they are also deeply humbling. Place a garden in the path of storm runoff and it's doomed to erode unless you plant accordingly. Bulbs are easily dislodged and sent floating. Mulch is doomed to be a washout and might impact your neighbors' property. On the other hand, ornamental grasses, with their deep roots, will hold firm and might forestall all of the bad stuff. Think about these things and take action before doing your rain dances.

A LITTLE NIGHT MUSIC

Y OU NEED A front porch. Beyond just being a place to proudly display the houseplant menagerie, the front porch is where you sit and rock after twilight, lulling yourself to snooze through those muggy, sultry,

When the sun finally sinks and the day's labor is over, the front porch waits for a weary gardener to listen to the surrounding serenade.

sleepless summer nights. It's the perfect venue from which to sample the smells of summer. But the porch (or the back deck) is also prime positioning for a concert. Under cover of darkness—lights squelched to dissuade mosquitoes and moths—your rocking chair moves slowly, rhythmically, back and forth, and you rest your weary self. You close your eyes, you try to doze. And you listen.

What you hear is the hypnotic cadence of midsummer's night music. It's a combination of maracas, sandpaper, and distant thunder. Remember Mungo Jerry's 1970's classic "In the Summertime"? The real thing is even more heady and compelling. The cicadas have an urgency that almost pulsates with sensuality. They do no major damage to plants, but if you hit the seventeen-year cicada cycle, it can become a din. Add the back-and-forth rhythm of katydid dialogue to cricket throbbing, and it's enough to turn up the heat. In summer, it can be soothing rather than eerie. There's comfort in knowing that all is going well in your surroundings.

While in Britain for a summer vacation, dead quiet woke me out of a deep sleep. The sound of total silence was terrifying. The cottage was in the middle of an agricultural field, and I don't even want to imagine how they secured the total lack of audio. But it gave me a newfound appreciation for my hometown bug band.

We take summer's night music for granted, but without vegetation the night sounds could be lost. Without woods and trees and fallen forest debris, the insects have no home. And where there are no insects, there are few birds. It's not really about being a gardener; it's about not gardening. In a community of carefully clipped lawns, there is no place for the serenaders of summer. Many insects that vocalize throughout summer nights reap the benefits of fringe habitats left in their natural state. It's more about neglect than cultivation.

Although fireflies are more of a visual phenomenon, they are critical to the outdoor experience. According to conservationist Doug Tallamy, their habitat is dwindling. But fireflies tend to hover over meadow-like fields. I leave my meadow completely unshorn throughout summer, and the resulting fireflies' flash-dance floating through the night could compete with anybody's choreography. Gardening is great fun, but sometimes you have to leave things to their own devices.

And then you need to experience the wonders that surround you. After you've left the fallen trees alone in the far depths of your property and you've neglected the unraked leaf litter by the wood's edge, find a place to sit outside in the night to celebrate the work you haven't done. You could settle onto a bench or a lounge chair somewhere outside. You could grope your way over to the gazebo or hunker down in the Adirondack chairs. But I suggest nestling into the rocker on the front porch. Just sit and listen to the night music. You've earned it.

Touch

TUG OF WAR

WHEN THE SUN isn't searing—in the early morning, in the evening, on cloudy days or alternate blue moons—you can safely tackle weeding. The weeds are the ones with the deep roots. You know you're dealing with a weed the moment it refuses to yield to your yank. If the plant clings ferociously to the earth, you can bet it's up to no good. Compare that stubborn grip to the adorable amsonia seedling that you newly discovered in just the right spot, much to your delight. One wrong move and you've unintentionally popped it out. Of course, not all cultivated plants have shallow roots and not all weeds plunge down with the tenacity of pokeweed. But numerous weeds are murder to remove.

However, tackling a stray weed in passing is never a good idea. You detect a lamb's quarters in the wrong place while headed past the garden for a night on the town. You're not wearing suitable footwear or gloves, but it seems one quick tug will efficiently dispatch the intruder. Wrong. You merely end up ripping the top off the weed in question, leaving the roots to send up a nastier, harder-to-pull weed in a few weeks. If you've ever tried removing burdocks (or any member of the sorrel family), purslane, carpetweed, or anything of similar ilk, you know what I mean. Wait until you can arm yourself with the weapons of warfare. Use tools to loosen the soil so the culprit is prime for the kill.

Sometimes it seems as though the Ho-Mi EZ-Digger is an extension of my arm, like I'm Captain Hook. This particular hand-forged tool goes under many names, but it's a curved-edged hoe used in Korea for thousands of years. You won't find me in the garden without it. The EZ-Digger is my personal favorite, but it's not the only weapon in town. Every gardener gets romantically attached to some sort of weeding tool that loosens the soil to ease the extraction process. If you haven't yet made that bond, you need to explore the field. The right tool is out there waiting for an

---

(FOLLOWING PAGE) No matter how vigilantly you patrol for weeds, they will come.

intimate relationship. You want something that won't balk at frequent (read: constant) use—nothing is worse than a weeding tool that breaks after a few swings. The apparatus should be easy to wield and equally efficient to aim—weeds love to wedge themselves into inconvenient crevices or nestle up too close to the good guys. Find a tool that can bite fairly deeply. I prefer a hand tool I can operate while crawling around because that's my typical battle stance. And a one-handed tool seems to work best, allowing me to dispatch the dastardly encroachers with my spare paw.

For really deep roots, like dock and all the peach seedlings that the squirrels have planted in the raised vegetable beds, I work with a transplanting spade made by Sneeboer in the Netherlands. It has a sharpened, V-shaped snake's tongue edge to the blade, like a giant dandelion weeder. And the long T-handle provides something on which to push down. I aim it, then step on the blade and persuade the taproot out. Or you might try a digging fork, which works for broad-rooted weeds like pokeweed. The fork gives you more leverage.

Arm yourself with something that means business. Once you have broken off the aboveground part without eliminating the roots of a weed, you've pretty much lost the battle—or at least prolonged the war. Gardening is really all about weeding and watering, with some planting on the side. For any of these chores, don't go in bare-handed.

LOVE SHOULDN'T HURT

GARDEN TOOLS INFLUENCE how you feel during and after gardening. Few of us think about tool grips at the point of purchase. We focus on the blade, the strength, the design, and whether it's going to get the work done. We spot that handsome shovel hanging in the shop, imagine it doing our bidding, and hire it for the job. It looks so sharp. It seems competent and well crafted. Metal is solidly merged into wood. Then you get the darn thing in your hands, dig in, and ouch!

It didn't take too many ouches for me to realize that T-handled shovels and spades are diabolically designed. They are fine for some applications, such as maneuvering a tenacious weed, but every job in the garden requires a dedicated tool. Digging has its own set of rules. Here's a common scenario: you're just beginning to tackle a project, you're full of spit and gung-ho, you arm yourself with that new T-handled shovel, you take aim for that first slice out of the soil, you hit the hard, unremitting earth with all your might, and you end up with carpal tunnel. T-handled shovels send all the impact of an action straight into your wrist like a shot. And we all know how easy it is to damage a wrist. You court disaster every time you hit the soil. And when you strike a stone (gardening in Connecticut, I figure that one out of every three shovel thrusts will result in a full-force interaction with a rock), it gets particularly painful.

As far as I can tell, poorly designed tools have existed throughout history. The tradition of spades with T-handles goes way back. Dyking and irrigation spades, Irish garden spades, and square shovels were notoriously designed with T-handles. But thoughtfully and safely designed tools also have a long precedent. If you are going to dig in, get yourself a Y-D handle.

Any time an action entails impact that might jar your wrist, a Y-D handle is the way to go. Rather than sending the impact straight to your wrist, a Y-D handle divides the repercussions into two sections, diffracting the shock. You grip a bar between the two sections so there is no direct hit.

I use what is called a ladies' shovel. It is a vintage tool with a gracefully arched swan neck and scaled-down proportions. In other words, it's built for someone my size, crafted when people actually were my size. Most men refuse to use it, as they might ruin their backs bending over to wield something that short. And that's another lesson: always take your height into account when purchasing tools. That half-size shovel might look quaint, but if you must bend over to make it work, your back is not going to be happy. Likewise for your leg muscles.

Speaking of pains, let's talk a little about watering cans. They can be a major issue during drought years, when it feels like the watering can

A T-handled tool (left) is not your best choice for high-impact chores.
A Y-D handle sends the shock away from your wrist.

is an appendage to your arm. For years, I lugged around heavy-duty vintage-type metal cans. I always toted two at once to balance the weight. But the day came when I switched to plastic, and I'm a better-adjusted person as a result. I go for the 5-liter Dramm watering cans because they are easy to fill and deftly designed not to tip forward. In addition, the water rarely sloshes out of the top, and the handles are slender for small grips (I have a very small grip), and designed beautifully for tipping. They have detachable roses (the many-holed nozzle at the end of the spout) that can be inserted when watering seedlings and removed when watering newly planted shrubs.

Everyone is built differently, and we need to take into account our own needs when outfitting ourselves for work. I always come equipped with my own tools when volunteering for a job so the experience is fully positive with no negative aftereffects. Take work seriously. Little pains can build up into major problems. If work begins to hurt, your tools might be the culprit.

PACE YOURSELF

H OW DO YOU step into the garden? If you're like me, you probably rush out, tool caddy in hand, as though your Muck Boots were on fire. A brisk trot is the understatement of the century. But now I set aside time for interaction at a whole different cadence. To relish the garden, you have to moderate your gait and adopt a slower pace.

Pathways are so important in a garden. It is easy to understand their role in transporting foot traffic from Point A to Point B in an efficient pattern. But sometimes we don't really get it on a deeper level. A good pathway makes moving around a garden a pleasurable experience and does more to further the adventure. Sometimes the fastest route is not the best one. If you want to immerse yourself in the garden, slow the tempo. Think about modulation in everything.

In a Japanese garden I first saw how syncopation could alter the pursuit of happiness. I was trying to plunge in at my usual vigorous stride, finding the going slightly obstructed, when our guide pointed to the path. That's when I noticed the raised stepping stones rather than one continuous paved progression. Had I been more keyed in, I would have sensed that the path was asking me to slow down.

Stepping stones are not necessarily the only way to go. Every pathway has a purpose, and it's not always just about convenience. Sometimes

A straightforward grassy path sends a walk-this-way message for a quick gait.
Stepping stones would slow the pace.

you want to direct attention to a particularly important bend in the path and what it's going to reveal around the corner. Sometimes you want to divert traffic flow around a focal point that's meant to steal your focus for a few extra minutes. The twisting, turning way might be the most fun. You might even want people to look down at what's happening at their feet—maybe a great groundcover or a precious little treasure they would miss if they weren't checking their footing. You might want to warn them to slow down when a footbridge is coming up. You might want to make moving around the garden as smooth, straightforward, and streamlined as possible.

Just watch your step. Think about it. Plan it. Most of us don't have expansive gardens, so we need to savor every inch of our little green space. Consider whether to leave it grassy, make it gravel, put in Belgian bricks, cobble it, set in stepping stones, or install pavers. You might put in something that diverts the flow instead of rushing right up to a destination. You could wind your route seductively to wherever it's going. You could smooth your pathway but consciously remember to take it slow. It's all in how you approach the garden. Only fools rush in.

SINKING IN

T HE MOSS AND I weren't always an item. In fact, I can remember when I marched around applying the ground limestone with determination, hoping to dispatch the moss from my domain. I was a new homeowner at the time, but I knew gardens and I knew lawn. What I didn't know was the many wonderful things that could happen in between. The moment I ceased the lawn liming, it was like someone gave the moss the go-ahead

There's nothing like sinking into a bed of moss in midsummer.
But did you ever truly get in touch?

to gallop out from the hinterlands and into the open arena. Ever since, I've fallen deeper and deeper in love. Now I kick myself for fighting the inevitable invasion of something glisteningly green, nearly indomitable, seductively spongy, all-encompassing, and maintenance-free.

In Connecticut, there is no way around the ledge. Not every property is equally stony, but you are invariably gardening between a rock and a hard place. Drive a stake in most anywhere on my seven acres, and you'll hit stone sooner rather than later. In the backyard, rocks dip and surface throughout the expanse, making it tempting to excavate and go the rock-garden route. But that would be tedious and expensive, and would require infinite patience. Plus, it would annihilate the moss. Apparently, the moss was always lurking there, waiting for the moment to reveal its true gallant colors. As soon as the soil was allowed to resume its naturally acidic pH, the moss rushed in. The beauty of rocks is that they sweat, increasing the moisture in the thin layer of soil covering them. The grateful moss has found its ideal ecosystem. Several species coexist in peaceful harmony. Sphagnum moss dwells beside other pioneer mosses to gradually displace the grass that struggles to survive. On the other hand, the moss remains green through drought and snow. As soon as the snow melts, it's already poised to spring back into spongy goodness. It looks great from a distance. It feels great up close. If I were the barefoot type, I would rip off my shoes to let it massage my soles. Instead, I just pat it lovingly every once in a while.

There's something very responsive about moss. At the very least, it's like a handshake. More accurately, it's a hug. When you step onto moss, you sink deep into the earth to be held closely in its folds. It's restorative. When you lie on moss, it's the closest you'll come to a total embrace. I know that moss can become a nuisance in the wrong places, and you can slip, slide, and hurt yourself when it invades your brick walkways. I completely understand why you would wage war against it in those circumstances for safety purposes and just to keep the traffic flow chugging along efficiently. But when moss moves into a lawn, I would favor the no-mow green carpet any day. It's just so much more luxuriant and interactive.

Some gardeners feed their moss a rich diet of buttermilk brushed on a stone's surface. My moss would probably flourish even more bodaciously given such indulgent treatment. But it is still doing astonishingly well. It has gradually spread along an entire wooded border of the property. It's now running beneath shrubs in a place that was formerly dicey mowing. It's like Emerald City.

Moss is one of the most hunkered-down, touchy-feely experiences imaginable. It's a whole different ecstasy than lawn, at a fraction of the upkeep. Life isn't always about easy conveyance from space to space. There are times when you want that sinking feeling, and moss is your greatest ally.

Taste

YOU SAY TOMATO

I DON'T ASK anyone to feel sorry for me because I'm ridiculously short. I don't beg for pity because my hair looks like I had a close encounter of the electrical kind. But I will accept sympathy on one point: I seem to be allergic to tomatoes.

When I eat tomatoes, consumption is followed by the pressing need to drink a few gallons of water, and the skin around my mouth is dry and cracked for the next few days. I was invited to a tomato tasting recently, and it put me right over the edge with stomach cramps, nausea, and the general feeling I was about to succumb to the Black Death. A friend had me on tomato lockdown for the rest of the summer.

Granted, tomatoes are the most tantalizing produce you are likely to pluck from your own backyard, with the possible exception of melons (which aren't so easy to grow—or safeguard from competitive nibblers). Thanks to their willingness to reside happily in containers, tomatoes are within the reach of everyone, no matter how little acreage you own. You can easily host tomatoes on your fire escape, if you don't mind climbing out the window with a watering can on a regular basis. And they are absolutely scrumptious, a trait that makes them infinitely more dangerous to me. They boast subtle innuendoes in taste and burst with the succulent goodness of lip-smacking juice. To bite into a ripe tomato snapped from its vine and popped straight into your mouth is a luxury not far from having your own private ice cream factory. Tomatoes are the relish of summer cut into slices, laid beside mozzarella, sprinkled with basil, and dribbled with balsamic vinaigrette. And tomatoes aren't even fattening—unlike chocolate and all the other temptations on the table. It's nothing less than tragic that I can't indulge.

Despite my handicap, I admit to planting a couple of tomatoes every year to share with friends. And a few slices sometimes somehow find their way into my salads (how does that happen?). I tend to grow the yellow versions that are lower in acid and I steer clear of paste, pear, and cherry tomatoes, which seem to wreak the most digestive havoc. I eat my pizza white and long ago swore off tomato bisque soup. I leave extreme tomato events to people who can tolerate higher acidity, while I grit my teeth and watch from the sidelines.

Tragically, fresh homegrown tomatoes might become a thing of the past. Hosting and harvesting tomatoes is an increasingly problematic feat because of early blight, late blight, fusarium wilt, powdery mildew, tomato mosaic virus, verticillium wilt, tomato apex necrosis virus, and more. The trick lies in finding and growing varieties with good disease resistance (check seed catalogs such as Johnny's Selected Seeds, which is quite forthcoming). Buy your tomato plants from a local nursery that starts its own plants from seed rather than purchasing from the garden-center department of a big-box store that ships them in. Or start your own from seed. Give plants plenty of space for air circulation, stake them up, and keep side shoots pruned, groomed, and off the ground. Not many predators filch tomatoes, but a murder of crows recently descended on the two token plants I was nurturing. I caught them red-beaked. The results were disastrous—for the tomatoes.

At tomato tastings, ironclad tummies try tomato after tomato and rank them for astringency, texture, taste, juiciness, pith, and balance of sweetness to acidity. I asked one particular tomato grower to share the results of his tastings. Benjamin Pauly, the master gardener who runs the Kelly Way Gardens, a culinary garden for The Woodstock Inn and Resort in Woodstock, Vermont, came up with his list of favorite tomatoes from his informal tallies. Best in show went to 'Aunt Ruby's German Green' (an heirloom beefsteak type from Tennessee that produces 1-pound green-yellow fruit with a pink blush when ripe); other standouts included 'Striped German' (a striped yellow-and-red 1- to 2-pound fruit with marbled interior), 'Yellow Brandywine' (an heirloom beefsteak type producing 1-pound yellow fruit), 'Green Zebra' (a particularly productive tomato with striped dark-green-and-yellow midsize fruit described as zingy in flavor), 'Cherokee Purple' (an heirloom that produces 12-ounce dark red fruit with green shoulders), 'Valencia' (a meaty heirloom with orange fruit weighing in at 8 to 10 ounces), and 'Esterina' (a miniature yellow tomato with high yields and flavor described as incredibly sweet with a tangy kick). As for me, I will just have to take his word for it, hand out the blue ribbons, and hope that I can someday indulge.

Ripe heirloom tomatoes are sunshine expressed in the form of fruit.

BERRY TANTALIZING

A GARDENER'S FRINGE benefits are many. Depending on where I'm standing in the yard, I will swear that whatever I'm seeing or whatever buzz I'm listening to is the greatest. The hand-to-mouth bursts of summer are as good as it gets. I defy any prince or demigod to be more fortunate than I am when the 'Chester' blackberries are ripe. And really, what bonus goes beyond the sheer luxury of plucking a few black currants and popping them into your mouth as you pass by the berry patch on the way to the barn?

The berry patch started out as a democratic endeavor. My goal was to please everyone. I would have the blueberries, gooseberries, and currants. The birds could peck all the viburnums and serviceberries they wanted. But the ratio was rejiggered. Apparently the feathered contingent didn't get the memo about the division of goods. One day I saw a male bluebird giving his missus a grand tour of the berry offerings on-site (not surprisingly, they set up housekeeping nearby). Ever since she discovered the buffet, the competition has been stiff for anything ripe and juicy, and innumerable bird species come to dine. My neighbor suggested that if I grew sufficient blueberries, the result would be plenty for everyone. But what the birds don't actually consume, they peck.

I have a system for beating the birds to the blueberries, but it ruins the spontaneity of growing your own berries. Netting is a lot of tangled inconvenience to install, and leads to substantial guilt when you find a poor winged thing tangled in the morning (heaven knows how long he was stuck). No matter how snug you try to fit the netting, they somehow find (or create) loopholes in the system. The result is mayhem. My solution is to skip the netting and go for constant vigilance. I get out at dawn and pick every single berry showing color. That takes the temptation

'Chester' blackberries are thornless (for painless harvesting) and scrumptious.

away. But I've tried to plant blueberries for the longest possible duration of harvest, so this equals considerable early-morning picking. From my crop of early 'Patriot' through midseason 'Bluecrop', late midseason 'Darrow' to late show 'Jersey', it's a race to get the ripe berries in the morning. It has led to black circles under my eyes and a lot of sour, not-quite-ripe berries in my yogurt. I'm researching caging and scary balloons sporting massive evil eyes.

The black currant crop has no such problem. Birds don't bother with black currants (*Ribes nigrum*). In fact, most people give them a wide berth. I love that burnt molasses-like taste. White pine blister rust can be an issue for currants and gooseberries, so I selected resistant varieties. 'Consort Black' and the large-berried 'Ben Sarek' qualify, and both are delicious.

Resistant red and champagne currants are bland by comparison, which endears them to the birds. Give me a black currant any day.

The problem with gooseberries as impromptu snacks is their nasty thorns. Chances are you'll get gruesomely scratched if you approach the most common white pine blister rust-resistant variety—*Ribes uva-crispa* 'Hinnonmaki Red'—without gloves. Besides that fault (and note that *R. uva-crispa* 'Pixwell' is a recent resistant variety without the barbs), gooseberries are a dead ringer for grapes, and like grapes, the fruit is scrumptious when it's slightly overripe. However, it's a fine line between when the fruit holds on the stems and when it drops to the ground. Another wrinkle: the birds quickly scarf up gooseberries the moment they land on the ground and thorns are no longer an issue.

Because I'm not overly fond of thorns, I've skipped raspberries. Instead, *Rubus fruticosus* 'Chester' fills the niche. This immense thornless blackberry bush has fat stems (it's billed as freestanding) and bears grape-size fruit on thornless brambles that wander hither and yon. Fruit production continues from early summer into autumn, and these are the biggest, juiciest berries you'll ever encounter. They have the crunchy substance typical of blackberries rather than the melt-in-your-mouth consistency of raspberries, but a handful on your way to picking broccoli for lunch is going to taste awfully good—if you can beat the birds to the prize.

LETTUCE STAND-INS

THERE COMES A sad juncture during every summer when lettuce cannot be convinced to grace my garden, let alone my table. No form of bribery is persuasive. Despite valiant efforts, lettuce seeds often refuse to germinate when the temperatures stay sizzling and parched for protracted days and weeks. Similarly, arugula—my favorite lettuce stand-in—runs up to seed in a blink. For salad purposes, I have to come

up with alternatives or else starve—in midsummer, I just don't see the supermarket as an option. That's where radicchio comes in.

Just when lettuce is in a heated snit, radicchio is performing. Admittedly, I originally trialed radicchio based on a flashy photo of the speckled 'Bel Fiore' in a Johnny's Selected Seeds catalog. It looked good enough to eat. However, initial taste tests were disappointing, but only because I tried devouring it too soon. Early on, radicchio tastes somewhat like bitter tissue paper. If you wait until 'Bel Fiore' has formed a nice tight head in

'Bel Fiore' radicchio goes from bitter to buttery when most lettuce is beginning to bolt.

late August or early September, it's a whole different culinary experience. The inner core goes from acrid to buttery and hits your taste buds more like lettuce and less like something that needs to be braised before it's edible. Not every radicchio makes it to this blissful level of perfection, sadly— some rot beforehand. But a survival rate of more than 50 percent ain't bad.

In early summer, when the lettuce is getting scarce, you might try plucking a few tender young, newly sprouted leaves of magenta spreen (*Chenopodium giganteum*) to flavor salads. Only the young tips on early summer growth are apropos; they get tough in no time. And moderation is the key—like many summer greens, these are high in oxalic acid, which is associated with kidney stones.

One of the handsomest vegetables you'll ever want to bite into, kale has ultra-frilly leaves that look like sea foam with a blue-green-purple cast. Most kales aren't really edible until autumn. But there are two exceptions newly on the market. The folks at Fruition Seeds pressed 'Bear Necessities' and 'Siber Frill' on me when I was dawdling around their booth at a flower show, and those two kales got me through a particularly hot, dry season. Although some kale is sold as microgreens for eating raw, these new introductions are tender throughout their life span. Keep them groomed by removing the lower leaves and you'll have something that could easily qualify as an ornamental. Although I tend to have an attitude toward vegetables that tickle going down, these two kales are not so hard to swallow.

You need all these edibles in your life. Part of the fun of a vegetable garden is growing sustenance that the grocery store can't supply. Sometimes you have to explore exotic fare. I doubt you will find many of these lettuce substitutes at your local market. But that's the beauty of growing for yourself. Your mouth enjoys privileged attractions. For foodies, it's totally worth it.

MAGIC BEANS

I DON'T USUALLY push vegetables on people. In general, my policy is you grow what you like, and I'll sow what I like. But somehow I've assumed the informal role of public relations advocate for 'Jade' bush beans. If you have a vegetable garden and don't want to hear the merits of 'Jade' beans, I suggest that you avoid contact with me in midsummer, or you will be exposed to a whole lot of pro-'Jade' propaganda.

Generally speaking, I'm brassica-centric. Although I'm not totally a cole-avore (you'll also find quantities of lettuce and plenty of squash on my plate), lunchtime tends to be predominated by broccoli, cauliflower, and that sort of thing. But when the 'Jade' beans start producing, suddenly the broccoli beds must vie for attention. Give me some quick boiled beans with a few leaves of freshly chopped basil for my noonday meal, and I'm a happy camper.

Recently, I mentioned this predilection when strolling through a restaurant garden with a chef. He looked down at me with an arched eyebrow just below his toque blanche and declared, "We do only filet haricots verts here." I'm sorry, but any vegetable that requires picking every thirty-six hours is not going to wash in my domain. No way am I going to become a slave to my beans. Give me a legume that can hold on the bush for several days without losing flavor and becoming tough.

If the chef had let me finish my spiel, I would have added that 'Jade' is capable of three crops from a single sowing—if you keep abreast of the harvest. During one hot and dry summer spate, I was on the road constantly, leaving 'Jade' to its own devices. Not only did the beans hold patiently for my return, but after I finally stripped the bush of its goodies, another flush of flowers and further beans followed. An opportunistic (and apparently gourmet) field mouse targeted one row of beans. But as soon as it was dissuaded from its gluttony, a mass of flowers burst forth from the truncated bushes. This bean just wants to make good.

Because 'Jade' has become a main staple (especially in midsummer when other vegetables are exhausted by the heat), I sow it every few weeks. When one row is busy getting its second wind, there's another crop coming. Meanwhile, the initial crop of 'Jade' beans, sown the first week of June, is still going strong the second week in September. The only trick is simultaneously producing enough basil to accompany the delish dish. Tender, juicy, crunchy, and flavorful, it doesn't get better than this. Did you bite into a bean today?

Behind a late-season lettuce, 'Jade' beans produce one of many crops.

Autumn

Don't dread autumn; embrace it.
If ever there was a season with a distinctive
mind of its own, autumn is that interlude.
Autumn is the time of the golden afternoons
and fiery sunsets. It's when your favorite
long-season crops finally ripen and the
meadow reaches its zenith.

There's a moment when the garden is outrageously
outfitted. But knowing that it will all fall soon,
who doesn't savor the show?

SPRING WORE A distinct wardrobe, and autumn also has its own dedicated outfits. Although irises now extend their performance to bloom sporadically during the growing season and peonies will probably also become more than just a spring affair, I hope nobody fiddles with asters and mums to switch their allegiance from autumn. If someone wants to create a precocious caryopteris to develop its blue blossoms at an earlier time of year, I'm not the least bit interested. Some of us relish the seasonality of gardens, and an autumn studded in oakleaf hydrangeas and lilac-colored callicarpa berries is what it's all about.

There is a hiatus in autumn—before the bulbs arrive, before the rakes are marshaled, when it's a little too late to put in new perennials but not time to start cleanup—that is custom made for honing your senses. Don't fail to savor your blessings. Do it now. Put your nose to the air to smell the telltale woodsmoke, go for a walk to find the wild grapes, invite some of autumn's more colorful personalities into your life, pick some apples. Autumn is fun. Sometimes it's blustery; often it's sweater weather. But autumn is frequently when we commune with our land. What I didn't call out in an essay for this book is the sound of sheer glee when we play outdoors. That pile of leaves, the pumpkin patch, the trick-or-treaters, and the tractor parades—they are all designed to get you outside, hooting and hollering.

But don't dawdle too long. Autumn has one undeniable personality trait: it is finite. You don't have all the time in the world. A lot of scrambling happens in late autumn. Along with the squirrels madly storing what they can stash away and butterflies taking one last sip of nectar before moving out or hunkering down, you have chores to accomplish. All I ask is that you don't blindly go about your duties. Everything can be more meaningful if you do it with eyes wide open.

Granted, this is the time when plants shed their clothes, but don't think of it as fall. When you engage with the season, be sure to work with it, bolster it, savor it. Autumn has riches galore.

Sight

BLADES OF GRASS

I T WAS Sydney Eddison who put plumes in my life. Of course, ornamental grasses were on my radar. You can't mingle in the horticultural realm without catching wind of the Oehme, van Sweden trend toward designing with grasses. Still, they didn't seem right for my decidedly retro cottage. Then Sydney stopped by and pointed out that my little world lacked any sort of nod in the Poaceae direction. No need to go wholeheartedly into grasses, she said, but how about sprinkling in just a representative or two? Not only does Sydney have impeccable taste, incredible design savvy, and an encyclopedic knowledge of plants, but she's also almost always right. You can—and should—dabble in design elements without going whole hog. I could (literally) see the wisdom in that advice. And of course she had a specific recommendation: *Miscanthus sinensis* 'Morning Light', right here," she said, standing in a spot that finished up a triangle with a magnolia and hydrangea. "It shines against the late afternoon light." I went to the nursery the very next day.

My reasons for holding grasses at arm's length weren't totally aesthetic. As a matter of policy, I avoid plants that require a lot of robust physical interaction, and grasses fall in that category. A few early brushes with fountain grass (*Pennisetum alopecuroides*) hybrids ended badly. When they began to grow scruffy (as grasses will do), I marched out armed with my trusty shovel to divide them up. Rather than giving you the full blow-by-blow account of the wrestling match that ensued, let's just cut to when I called in a crew of musclemen to eliminate the deep-rooted plants permanently (and I'm talking tenacious roots that plunged several feet down). I couldn't even find anyone willing to accept donated divisions. Fountain grass can be a bear.

As the weather turns colder, the blades of *Miscanthus sinensis* 'Morning Light' begin to curl along with the plumes. The result is breathtaking.

But Sydney didn't steer me wrong. So far, 'Morning Light' has been a laudable citizen. It plays well with others and hasn't caused even a tinge of back pain. Although all grasses are slow out of the starting gate in spring, by summer 'Morning Light' has formed a nice tight cluster of pencil-thin, white-banded grayish leaves that dance when the cars spin past. Long before the pink and then burgundy plumes appear, 'Morning Light' is busy making an architectural statement. It is the perfect foil for the point where the driveway meets the road. With a peppering of some *Sanguisorba officinalis* 'Red Thunder' (thank you, Opus Plants) to jazz up the statement before the plumes, it's a happy marriage.

The relationship gains another layer when autumn flowering time draws near. It's a slow drama as the tassels unfold, and then it's a protracted triumph while the plumes stand tall and wave at passersby (an interlude that coincides nicely with the town's tractor parade). Gradually, the whole shebang blanches flaxen, catching the sinking sun as it happens earlier and earlier each week. The blades turn color and somehow gyrate with frosty weather—each corkscrewing blade creating an artistic spin. I wish I could hold that thought throughout the winter, but the pangs of neighborly obligation strike. Around here, the first snow can arrive before the solstice, bringing with it a convoy of overly energetic plowmen who have been chafing at the bit to move mountains—or break grass blades into smithereens. They deposit the wealth from my 'Morning Light' all over the neighborhood. And everyone knows from whence that litter came. Before the inevitable happens (sometimes hours before a storm is predicted), I cut the grasses down. I apologize to the vehement contingent of the leave-the-garden-intact-through-winter movement. Maybe I'm depriving some poor creature of winter fluff for its den. But the bird or beast in question should have planned its housekeeping strategy sooner. And it can always rifle through the debris in the compost heap.

Grasses are the current buzzword in gardening for the discreet screen they lend a garden and the textural interplay they afford mingled with fellow plants. Who can blame you for falling in love? But many grasses have bad habits. After inviting *Achnatherum brachytricha* into my life, it looks like seedlings will be haunting me into eternity, despite attempts to remove the plumes shortly after they crest and before they scatter seeds. My neighbor asked for a clump, which furnished the opportunity to be very generous, but I was surprised that he didn't already have half a dozen. He will be rolling in many of its children shortly. Northern sea oats (*Chasmanthium latifolium*) is also notoriously plentiful with its issuance. And then there's the long-term upkeep. Even if all goes well, good-citizen tall grasses (the clump-forming sedges are an exception) eventually become hollow in the center of the clump, requiring digging and dividing to retain their handsome state. But no one can blame gardeners for becoming enamored. Nothing compares to feathery tassels catching the low light of autumn. It's a beautiful sight, and might be worth the extra labor.

TAKING LEAVE OF YOUR SENSES

F LASHY VARIEGATED LEAVES aren't really my thing. The white-striped 'Morning Light' miscanthus is about as garish as it gets around here. Be my guest and indulge in the carnival-hued red, green, and cream *Cornus florida* 'Daybreak' or the rainbow-leaved *Fagus sylvatica* 'Tricolor' in your yard. I'll come over and applaud. But don't send me home with one for my garden. In summer, my strategy is to let the flowers cause the stir and keep the background music fairly quiet. Besides a deep burgundy-leaf *Cercis canadensis* 'Forest Pansy' and a few deep wine ninebarks (*Physocarpus* cultivars) the color scheme is fairly subdued for the woody contingent at Furthermore. However, that cool, calm, and collected stance changes dramatically in autumn.

The beauty of autumn lies not only in its fervor but also in its syncopation of events. One reason to love autumn is that it strings you along. Autumn doesn't hit all at once. There is a gradual cadence to the denouement that demands continual vigilance if you don't want to miss a beat. The whole shebang is layered, and everything is meticulously timed. It is nature's version of sound bites. Each plant comes onstage, presents its colorful skit, and bows out. The amsonia and a few other long-winded performers remain radiant over the long haul. But most of autumn's

performers do a flashier bit, then move on to the striptease in short order. It's thrilling.

The excitement begins up high. As soon as September melts into October, the trees send out initial hints about their intentions to go out in a blaze. From there, the slow-moving fire ignites the shrubs. The sumacs are among the first to give notice, going to a riveting orange before summarily turning an unflattering, downright depressing shade of brown-black. Remove their browned leaves immediately, because those sad remnants will hold on for dear life. No need for negativity. Keep autumn upbeat by whisking protagonists offstage when they go bedraggled. The sumacs are followed in short order by hydrangeas burnishing bronze and yellow, with several viburnums eventually chiming in to blush burgundy. A week later, the hydrangeas will be dropping leaves while *Amsonia hubrichtii* slips into a fetching orange outfit. Underfoot, the geraniums have gone all festive with orange and bright red leaves. By then, the surrounding sugar maples are getting into the seasonal spirit and the magnolia is just beginning to bleach yellow. When Halloween rolls around, the redbud has swung into action, deciduous azaleas are staging their last hurrah, potentillas are following suit, the Japanese maples are raging, the spireas are joining in but relatively demure compared to the neon red of the mountain sumac (*Rhus copallinum*)—which trails other sumacs timewise but explodes with a color that's worth the wait. That's the curtain call. By Election Day, the circus is moving out of town with few vestiges left besides Japanese maples that refuse to concede and some flaxen amsonia that will hold firm for another month.

That's just the quick roll call. Meanwhile, the bordering color of leaves clinging to the trees in the surrounding forests will float down or be stripped naked in a violent windstorm. Even that is a feast for your eyes. The confetti of colorful leaves looks lovely until raking reality strikes, requiring you to somehow get those leaves out of the garden before they turn into a sloppy mess, invade the neighbors' space, and ultimately impede spring's progress. Don't give me the leave-the-leaves-where-they-fall bit. Yes, you can chop them up and reapply, but a mess of

Ornamental kales like 'Pigeon Red' are wonderfully inexpensive delights.

huge maple or sycamore leaves is not going to lead to simple peace and harmony with the people next door.

I'm all for letting the show unfold while staying attuned. That's why I don't hack the asters back even after the last cobalt blue flower has flagged. There is some color in those leaves yet. The amsonia is probably the perennial performer of longest duration, but columbines, stokesia, carex, armeria, and hakonechloa stage their moment in the sun and are left standing to linger as long as possible. Herbaceous peonies turn outrageous shades. And let's not discount the so-called flowering kales and cabbages that flood the market in autumn. Their purple leaves are the perfect counterpoint to the foliar fury of oranges. No matter which one you choose (and there's no point in listing names, because new introductions will be popping up annually), flowering kales and cabbages are absolutely worth the meager price tag that garden centers affix to these workhorses. They are stunning wonders of nature (with more than a little help from humans).

You don't want to take your eyes off the garden for a nanosecond. You don't want to miss a moment. The good news is that autumn cleanup sends you outside at regular intervals. Take the excuse to rake, prune, and groom while watching what's going down. This is no time to leave town.

THE BLUES

I F YOU THOUGHT this was where I'd start whining about summer's departure, you are dead wrong. As much as everyone loves summer, autumn stands on its own merits and offers plenty of fodder for astute senses. The carnival of autumn foliage is the obvious highlight of the season, but you can turn up that action several decibels by playing your

Despite their relatively small dimensions, aster flowers read well in autumn, even at a distance, thanks to their popping blue hues.

combinations right. Radiant autumn foliage is a generous gift from nature, and maximizing that endowment is what a garden is all about. Here's where you can work complements and apply your magic to bring the garden up to another level.

What you really need in autumn is a good case of the blues. I mean that literally. Juxtaposed against all those flaming oranges, reds, and yellows that the season hands out, the polar opposite of the color spectrum reads like never before. Granted, spring sprouted with a gush of blue, but this is a whole different hue. Autumn gives you a spectrum in the more royal purple and azure sphere compared to the cobalt and cornflower of spring. Plus, in autumn we have surround-sound. In spring, we lacked the all-encompassing volume compared to the bulked-up girth galore of autumn. There is more of everything on the playing field.

Blues sort of sink into the horizon in summer. Under the beating sun, they are prone to read as a listless shade of mauve or disappear as a dark tone of navy. But autumn light is a whole different ball game. When the sun is lower in the sky, the rays ignite richer colors. Autumn sunsets backlight your garden. You can put on the spotlight from behind, accentuating individual players. Your plants will be set on fire. And the sun sinks down earlier every day for the performance. What once appeared to be a midnight hue is transformed into sapphire in autumn. Meanwhile, the flaming foliage of the surrounding tree line is also part of the conspiracy.

Asters are the obvious route, but take that familiar road anyway. Asters richly deserve all the ovations they have earned. I refuse to humor the sadistic nomenclaturists who slapped the name *Symphyotrichum* on this poor unassuming group of plants. They'll always be asters. And more asters are being introduced into cultivation each year. I'm just as wild as everyone else about the little buns they sell in the nurseries, such as *S. novae-angliae* 'Purple Dome'. They are the cat's meow. But what about your disappointment when last year's front-of-the-border bun stretches into a leggy eyesore with brown foliage from the waist down? And no matter when you prune, you just can't get the stiff-stemmed New England asters to look presentable. Instead, turn to *S. oblongifolium* selections—'Raydon's Favorite' is a long-lasting, cheerful blue late bloomer that manages to keep itself tidy and clothed from head to toe. Producing arching 3-foot stems, it fills a whole different position in the border compared to the *S. novae-angliae* cultivars. But it still turns heads. *Symphyotrichum oblongifolium* 'October Skies' is a close second for the blue beauty contest. Even taller is *S. laeve* 'Blue Bird', clocking in at 4 feet and equally lusty. They aren't front-of-the-border plants, but at least they don't pretend to fill that niche. Instead, they are wonderfully giddy in the middle or back of the border. Celebrate their talent.

We associate asters with autumn because they see out the season, but there are plenty of blue bloomers in early autumn that bridge the gap and complement the first plants to turn color, like amsonia and hydrangeas. I'm thinking of monkshoods, eryngiums, gentians, *Lobelia siphilitica*, *Lithodora diffusa* 'Grace Ward', caryopteris, *Ceratostigma plumbaginoides*, *Phlox paniculata* 'Nicky' or 'Blue Paradise' (a personal favorite), and maybe even a second blooming in your nepetas, delphiniums, and salvias (if you cut back immediately after the initial flowering). They work equally brilliantly pitted against the orange backdrop of autumn. They bring the season over the top.

And after all, gardening is all about creating magic moments. Nature gives us wonderful gifts, and gardeners take those blessings and run with them. Try running in the blue direction, much to your eyes' delight.

GONE TO SEED

A UTUMN IS SEEDY. (And who can figure how that word acquired such a negative connotation?) This is when plants slip into parental mode and plan their progeny. This is when plants invest in the future of the planet. How could that be ugly?

Look closely, and you'll realize that seedheads are fascinating. Although they aren't usually as glam as flowers, they are intricate little packets carefully designed to ensure a tomorrow for whatever sedum, mountain mint, aster, marigold, or echinacea they plan to disperse. Generally they have faded to flaxen or varying shades of tawny by the time

autumn rolls around. Whatever holds them to their momma has become paper-thin in preparation for launching the kids into a world of their own. Anise hyssop seedheads have bracts like snakeskin. Eryngium seedheads have an intricacy that rivals any Hollywood rendition of a spaceship. Milkweed and butterfly weed pods are arguably more alluring than the flowers that got them into their motherly condition in the first place. With some autumn sun glinting on their shells, they have that maternal glow while sowing their family to the winds on gossamer parachutes. Seeing a milkweed disperse is a silken fairy-tale moment that is pure magic. If a humble seed could ride such a glorious sail, anything is possible.

Of course, not all seeds are welcome. Anything you can do to dissuade Japanese knotweed from investing in dividends is a wise move. Although their paper-thin, dangling seed packets sparkle in the low autumn morning light, they spell nothing but trouble. I secretly sneak over to my neighbor's property line and cut the flowers to feed to the goats before they can become mothers to thousands. Similarly, you want to rogue out all the Chinese forget-me-nots (*Cynoglossum amabile*) and burdocks (*Arctium minus*) you can possibly eradicate long before they form the seeds that catch at your clothing, become hitchhikers, and make total nuisances of themselves. The flowers are handsome (especially on bright blue cynoglossum), but cut them down while still in the blossom stage—or pay the price in ruined sweaters.

Autumn is not only about the tawny and flaxen seedpods that remain after perennials have given up for the growing season. Nature found other ways to package potential progeny. Rose hips and berries are also rewards for those who don't obsessively tidy up. Even the old standby 'New Dawn' makes a few token hips. But other roses are valued specifically for that trait. Rugosa roses are so bristly that we aren't apt to deadhead without donning battle armor, so we tend to delay, which is good news for developing rose hips. But other roses also follow suit. I asked Michael Marriott of David Austin Roses to shout out a few roses favored for their good hips, and he suggested 'Rambling Rector', 'Francis E. Lester', 'The

Nothing is more poetic than the choreography of a milkweed shedding its gossamer seeds.

Generous Gardener', 'James Galway', 'Penelope', 'Windrush', and 'Carefree Beauty'. For species roses with boutique-worthy hips, he mentioned *Rosa moyesii* (pear-shaped) and *R. glauca* (purple). And for North American native species with long-lasting hips, Michael suggested *R. virginiana*, *R. californica*, and *R. woodsii*. Roses certainly aren't the only shrubs to take that packaging route aimed at enticing birds to help with seed dispersal. Other shrubs and vines slip into the serious business of producing berries. Some of the noninvasive honeysuckles bear a few wonderful glistening berries on their meandering vines. Many viburnums have drupes in varying colors. Autumn is downright fruitful.

Keep seedheads for as long as you can. Remove them only when they threaten to litter the neighborhood in an early-season snowstorm. Not only do the birds applaud this policy, but it also keeps the garden happening as long as possible. And it secures a future for enterprising perennials prone to self-sow. All those seeds (assuming they are "good guys") spell money saved, if you play your cards right and let them sprout. At this time of year, seedy is exactly what you want in a scene.

BROWN IS BEAUTIFUL

IN SUMMER, brown is the disappointment. In autumn, brown is the reward. While thinking of seed, brown is most beautiful when it gangs up together. It's a matter of volume. One brown branch in a vast sea of green needs an apology. When the entire canvas fades brown and even the last aster turns tawny, brown gets the respect it deserves. Suddenly, the picture is seen in sepia, translated into various shades of auburn highlighted by a cinnamon or cocoa accent dappling here and there. Our

It's a toss-up: does *Hydrangea paniculata* 'Quick Fire' look best in summer with its pink-tinged sterile flowers or when brown in autumn?

eye scans for an occasional burgundy flash, while the rest of the scene is toast. Pessimists would call it drab, but they're not gardeners. We search for the silver lining. And sure enough, there's a subtle majesty when ochres are highlighted by glittering frost as Jack completes his etchings every morning. Truly adept gardeners work their browns, stacking the taupe against the chestnut and balancing the fawn beside the ginger. Skillful colorists silhouette the sedums in front of the amsonia to maximize the late show. They bask in their browns.

Around here, brown isn't the consolation prize. There's nothing melancholy about buff in autumn. Volume gives texture to the weave. By autumn, you've built up so much heft that the brown becomes a woolly blanket before your eyes. It's not just a lone bit of brown, it's a conversation. That dialogue is the goal for gardeners who strive to extend their seasons beyond the obvious frost-free dates.

Further toward this lofty aspiration, there's a movement afloat advocating density planting, where everything is nestled so closely cheek by jowl that the soil isn't a visible factor. Plant fanatics who keep jamming new acquisitions into a finite space have been practicing this method for decades. Now we have a label for it. Density planting really shines in shades of brown with maybe some striking evergreens dappled around for definition and a few blue-gray herbs (I'm looking at *Salvia officinalis* 'Berggarten' right now) as a frame of reference. In mid-December, it's ravishing.

The meadow is density planting at its finest. Most gardeners call out late summer as a meadow's shining hour, but I disagree. When my goldenrod and Joe Pye weed turn brown, that's their runway moment, especially when the whole nubby weave is garnished with the sparkling sugarcoated frosting that melts your heart. Something about the unison of color has a striking richness that draws in your eye and begs for closer examination. It's a symphony. And when you think about it, everything in that meadow is now focused on the heavy-duty responsibility of producing seeds for the next generation. It's like the whole meadow is united in the lofty mission of securing a future. It has earned its depth.

I keep the volume high as long as possible. It's a tricky balance. Every day, I look out at my garden from the windows, from the driveway, from the road, from wherever I happen to be working on the property, from all angles, and assess it. Does it look like harmony or a maintenance lapse? Does it look happy or neglected? Then the paring down ensues. It's never a clean sweep. Instead, I make swipes at the scene to take out one element or another that's looking ill-kempt. Maybe the sweet William needs to be cut back, but the eryngium still looks great. Maybe the echinops is breaking apart, but the echinacea is standing strong. I leave as much as possible for birds or those who need to forage. But whenever I cut something down, my labors are followed by a cleanup crew of juncos, titmice, and chickadees with perhaps a stray blue jay or cardinal as sidekicks. There is no waste here.

Consider spot removal in autumn rather than total eradication. Editing gradually leads to the same svelte results, but you gain maximum impact along the way. The unique feature of this season is that it remakes itself daily. Never accuse autumn of being monotonous. You wake up to something that's been stripped of leaves in a tailwind. You look out at dusk on something blushing a brighter shade, or blanched a paler hue, or torn asunder in an early-season flurry. And you remake the scene around the new dialogue. Autumn is dynamic. Don't banish your brown prematurely. Celebrate it. Brown is not the tragedy; brown is the happy ending.

Smell

GRAPE NUTS

Y OU SUSPECTED AUTUMN was in the air. Maybe you even feared fall's inevitable arrival. But you didn't come to grips with the change of season until you were walking—maybe where the woods meets the edge of a field, or somewhere on a dirt road—and a slight breeze brought the hint of wild grapes wafting to your nose. Wild grapes announce that fall is inevitable. I can't think of a more seductive way to wrap up the growing season. Grapes are a good argument for embracing fall and all its many blessings.

Wild grapes ease you into autumn. Something about that fresh scent is so fully satisfying, it goes beyond the Bacchus-laden baggage that grapes have acquired and adds a personal identity to the interchange. That heady, high-pitched, sticky-sweet, maybe even slightly sour bouquet floating lightly on the air whispers that wild grapes have laced through the undergrowth and are producing the spoils of their crop. I'm always amazed that the birds haven't pecked them into oblivion and black bears haven't stolen their fill long before I catch wind of the bounty. There is invariably an opportunity to follow my nose to some wild grapes. It's a little like a treasure hunt.

Beyond declaring the official denouement of the growing season, wild grapes remind us to leave it be. Gardening is grand, but not gardening is just as critical to the balance of nature as cultivated areas. We are all proud of nice and tidy. But we need to set aside no-man's-land as well. Maybe the terrain where grapes have snuck in is not the place you fuss over and nurture with the fanatical servitude that you bestow on your garden, but it's a valid ecosystem nonetheless. It sends out its scents, sustains a whole slew of critters, provides provisions for innumerable insects, and generally keeps the balance in check. As a gardener, you have the duty to support that land.

(FOLLOWING PAGE) In autumn, wild grapes are steeped in the other scents of the season.

Folks have a love-hate relationship with wild grapes. They can wreak havoc with the trees that they use to get a leg up, stealing their sunbeams and adding weight. After timbering, their seeds can sit in the soil for years, waiting for the right moment to germinate. Foresters aren't overly fond of a fruit that they see as a menace to their arboreal crop. But I greet wild grapes as part of the overall sensual experience. They're here, they're hard to dissuade (cutting back the vines just leads to later sprouting), and they provide provisions for the throng of creation beyond our sphere of control. To keep it all happening, we need the sort of spaces that grapes frequent. Some places should remain beyond our domain. By all means, walk by those areas and remain cognizant of their gifts. Breathe in and feast your eyes, but resist the urge to impact them. Some blessings are best left alone.

BLOWING IN THE WIND

I WAFFLED ABOUT where to discuss autumn winds, because fall is all about blistery gusts that send the leaves scurrying around and whip your leaf-raking tarp right out of your hands. They scatter whatever you're doing into the neighbor's yard. They blow debris into your eyes, sting your face, and tingle your hands. When wind comes in the gentler, breezier, more user-friendly form, it fans those wild grapes to your senses. Its breath caresses your cheek, ruffles your hair, and refreshes your brow as you haul all those cherished annuals indoors and escort the frost-nipped basil to the compost. It dries the tears. There is definitely a tactile element to the wind.

Wind is also very audible. It's particularly vocal in winter, when all its various obstructions are laid bare and it can howl to its heart's content. That's the bombastic, swaggering wind that goes screeching around like a teenager in a fast car. But the wind croons in autumn as well. The sounds aren't nearly as blustery. In autumn, wind makes more of a sweeping set

of sounds while fingering the earth. It does a little whoosh here and a little dash there. Most of what we hear is not the wind, but the objects it shuffles around. The scuttling of leaves, the twitch of touching branches, the whip of dangling twigs is the audio that accompanies wind. Secure everything. Go around with your ears perked and monitor for loose ends. Autumn can serve as a fire drill for winter.

Wind in autumn also sends scents rushing around. It's like public transportation that fast-tracks smells from the source. On chilly evenings, it delivers the first waft of woodsmoke to your nose. Even if you were

The fresh scent of laundry is like no other aroma in autumn.

blindfolded, that telltale whiff would inform your senses that autumn is in the air. It's different from the light smell of summer's campfires. Instead, autumn puts its own distinct inimitable, signature stamp on the scent. It's not pouring out and it's not full of sparks. Instead, it comes fanning in and promises to tingle your senses for several months to come. Chimney smoke differs markedly from the rank smell of burn piles. In autumn, perceiving the scent from the hearth is one of the most comforting, hunkered-down aromas in the world. You want to follow it and sit beside the fireplace with a mug of mulled cider warming your chilled bulb-planting fingers. The smell of woodsmoke gives you the second wind to wrap up the job at hand and be embraced by the coziness of a crackling fireplace.

Woodsmoke is wind's obvious hitchhiker, but other aromas also catch a lift. Maybe there is an undercurrent of evergreens with musky leaves incorporated in spaces where you haven't reconnoitered for months. Sometimes it's the essence of soil that has been dislodged during raking or a whiff of the moss that's growing by the forest's edge. The wind delivers the message, tattling on what's been hidden and outing buried treasures. In autumn, various mushrooms announce their presence after being dislodged from wherever they're lurking—sending up that musky forest scent of something grumbling at being disturbed by emitting an ever-so-slightly foul rebuke. On a mild day, the different air currents send up plumes of perfume as they mingle. Put your nose to the wind, and the result can be evocatively sensational as well as informative. You know your garden on a whole different level, like the street-smart cat who pauses at the door to sniff the air before venturing out. All sorts of shorthand is written on the wind. For the cat it could be life or death. For the gardener, it could be revelations about yet another chore added to the agenda (if, say, some varmint discovered and ravaged the bag of deer repellent). What the wind carries on its shoulders is a telling narrative for a gardener.

The wind can also be an ally getting the work done. The wind is an energy-saving, totally sustainable resource that can do our bidding. In autumn, the clothesline is called into action on a regular basis. Not only does it harness the wind and its energy to work its magic on the sheets, but it also infuses whatever was hung with a fulsome fresh scent that is the polar opposite of any commercial perfumed product. No matter what smell they incorporate into washing detergents, it will never hold a candle to the breath of a piece of laundry snatched from the line on an autumn evening as the sun sinks down. It's fresh. It's real. It's local. It smells like home. While rushing the laundry indoors, bury your face in your newly laundered clothes and breathe in. When you dab your damp body with the towel and then sink into the bedsheets that night, take a minute to inhale deeply. That's the reward from the wind.

DEERLY DEPARTED

I'VE BEEN RHAPSODIZING about roses and ranting over wild grapes. We've talked about lilies and all manner of other delights for your sense of smell. But here comes the reality check. Unless you have a deer fence and a magical method for keeping the bunnies at bay, none of those scents is going to fill your garden with undiluted aroma. There is a smell that is universally shared among all gardens that aren't wrapped prophylactically in a fence. Somewhere in the configuration, there will be an undercurrent of animal repellent. It is hard for a rose's aroma, no matter how redolent, to stand a chance against the blaring miasma of Bobbex.

I must admit, I sort of like the essence of deer repellent. Certainly, a mélange of fermented fish and rotten eggs possibly combined with hot pepper and garlic is nobody's version of heaven for the nose. Some deer and rabbit repellents rely on dried blood. Others plug in coyote (or other predator) urine. These solutions share only one trait: none is going to please your next inhale. But for many of us, this is a necessary precaution. That rose is not going to smell like anything if it is nibbled from the vine. This is just one of the cold, hard facts of gardening in the age of predators who have inadequate forage at their disposal and too many juicy beds to access. From their point of view, we've taken away their wild browsing areas and planted cafeterias instead.

Of course, the worst olfactory moment is right after you've sprayed. I suggest going shopping or finding some other excuse to vacate the prem-

ises immediately. A great time to spray is before leaving on vacation, but only if those who remain at home are in agreement. And it's wise to fill them in on your scheme so they don't suspect foul play. We've all heard of the skunk at the garden party.

I find that the stinkier sprays are most effective, and that it's a good strategy to switch up your formula. Self-preservation is such a strong urge that deer (and other browsers—the bunnies are also on a rampage) become accustomed to a scent. That's why it works to confuse the issue with several

I douse the prince's feather (*Amaranthus cruentus*) surrounding the upper vegetable garden with deer repellent in lieu of a fence.

products, switching repellents every few weeks. You may begin to wonder if the nibblers come to realize that anything that smells like rotten eggs is particularly tasty, so try broadcasting the spray beyond the hostas and other plants that witness the worst deer pillage. I spray almost everything. That keeps them guessing (while simultaneously totally fudging any good scents that the garden might be emitting). Perhaps most important, you need to spray from spring onward. Once deer have discovered roses, they know that a delicious meal ticket is lurking beneath the stinky stuff. I have discovered the hard way that pepper spray—and anything else that uses taste as a prohibiting signal—does not work at all. Once a deer has a goody in its mouth, that plant is gone. Smell is a better deterrent.

Is floral fragrance a thing of the past? Not really. After you've sprayed your garden with repellent, you can still come in for the close encounter with a rose blossom and inhale its lovely aroma. Ditto for fragrant hosta blooms as well as lily petals. The overall malodorous stuff adds another note, but the experience up close and personal of a newly opened and yet unsprayed bud is still heaven. And deer repellent dissipates with time (at which point you should apply it again). Or you could put up a deer fence and have the full rapture untainted. That might be the way to go on all levels and for all your senses. A garden ravaged is not a pretty sight, smell, taste, or feel. And nobody likes the sound of predators running away with a mouthful of your favorite delicacy clenched in their teeth.

Sound

NOT COUNTING CROWS

THERE ARE MANY hints that autumn is coming. From the preponderance of woolly bear caterpillars lethargically inching along the garden pathways to berries forming on the neighbor's poison ivy, the cues are numerous. When the bumblebees are slower to rally in the morning and dusk follows afternoon too closely, you get the first inklings that autumn is creeping in. But if you put your ear to the ground, you can also detect some undeniable indicators of the seasonal change. Here at Furthermore, the ruckus irrefutably signals that fall is nigh.

Except where my land fell into the water sometime after they drew the parcel map more than a century ago, I don't own the pond (aka Lake Lauriat). But I consider myself to be its partial steward, and my senses certainly benefit from the wildlife that congregates around it. In summer, various ducks and an occasional swan glide around enjoying the vegetation. By autumn, the diversity has thinned dramatically until the pond becomes the sole hangout of the Canada geese. Every evening, they sail in for a landing with a fanfare announced with a series of honks that would rival taxis jostling for lanes on the George Washington Bridge at rush hour. It's loud enough to startle houseguests. They ask if we can turn on the radio and listen for directions to the nearest bomb shelter from the Emergency Alert System. But to me, it just sounds like home in autumn.

I'm strictly a novice backyard birder, so the Canada geese and their vocalizations were one of the only bird behaviors I really noticed. When I began to pay more attention, I realized that many birds are nearly as talkative in autumn as they are during spring mating season. In particular, my meadow becomes the social gathering place for flocks of birds. They swoop in, hold conventions, feast on the wildflowers shedding their seeds, and move on to make way for the next party of revelers. Apparently, according to the experts, all those strange goldenrod galls in the meadow harbor fly larvae. What looks like a plant health issue is actually an essential source of fat and protein for chickadees, titmice, and downy woodpeckers. I asked Ray Belding—member of the Litch-

field Hills Audubon Society, avid birder, and frequent binocular-bearing expert on many things feathered—to give me the skinny on what goes on in autumn. He generously translated all the conversations on which I was eavesdropping.

"They're vocal," Ray agreed about the geese. "Although they nest in pairs, they flock together in autumn." And apparently there is plenty to quack about while traveling. "If a member of the flock dies, they leave his space open in the V for several days. While traveling, they often land in farm fields to eat." He was impressed that the Canada geese hadn't

---

Ever notice that the crows appoint a sentinel bird to stand guard?

waddled their way beyond the pond's edge into my lawn and meadow after cutting. I think we can thank the dense vegetation around the pond's edge for keeping the geese and their droppings out from underfoot. Manicure the outer edges of your property, and problems arise. My laissez-faire approach to land stewardship keeps the pond habitat at a respectful distance. I have a view corridor, but I leave the scrub unmown around the periphery. Even if we don't live together in simple peace because of the honking that ensues whenever the geese perceive a threat (real or imagined), we do coexist in harmony.

The geese are only part of the dialogue among feathered factions. Most of the other discussion is between what Ray calls "black birds," the darkly plumed birds that tend to congregate in autumn when preparing for migration. He explained that there is no specific blackbird native to the United States besides the red-winged blackbird. Common grackles, brown-headed cowbirds, red-winged blackbirds, and starlings all group together in autumn. By sheer numbers (Ray described flocks in the thousands), you are bound to hear about it. The starlings in particular congregate in astonishing numbers and perform their beautifully choreographed aerial stunts, called murmurations. Scientists say they are reacting to a potential hawk or predator, leading it on a merry chase. To us, it seems they are reveling in the sheer joy of synchronized flight. They can become a nuisance, and the sound of their chattering after settling down probably inspired Alfred Hitchcock's psycho-thriller. Too many of anything can be deafening. But consider their lilting dance as it swoops and glides and swirls, gyrating through the sky, and it compares favorably with any theatrical performance. And from an audible standpoint, most other flocking black birds don't amass in equal numbers. What you usually hear in autumn is the chips, call notes, and squawks that birds use in their general chitchat. "At dusk, they're reporting the location of each bird," Ray explained. Rather than the romantically melodic amorous, aggressive, and territorial trilling during spring mating season, this is about group solidarity.

Eventually, the departing flights take off. Warblers leave first, followed by other snowbirds heading for milder climes. Red-winged blackbirds and Swainson's thrushes migrate at night. Even in pitch dark, Ray can identify who's flying above by the call notes. But they don't all abscond. Several birds that previously migrated now remain, thanks to climate change. American robins often stay in our area, ruining the fun of marking their return in spring. That would explain why I find them bingeing on berries. "But during a winter thaw, they can also find worms in the moist earth," Ray explained. Cedar waxwings are also prone to overindulgence, according to Ray. But they are more apt to share the spoils in winter, which explains the peacefully coexisting groups of birds hanging out together without incident. The mourning doves are an exception. Ray has noticed that they don't even tolerate other mourning doves.

The crows are a different matter entirely. A murder of crows noisily goes about its bad-boy behavior with constant heckling and snide remarks. In autumn, they swagger around my freshly cut meadow talking about everything from the seed harvest to the weather. They know me now, and usually just take a few token steps out of my way when I walk by, while expressing their general displeasure at my appearance and their disdain for whatever I'm doing. The feeling isn't actually mutual (except when they help themselves to my tomatoes). I find their presence mildly comforting, figuring it means no harm is lurking nearby.

When I began to listen, I realized that the bird soundtrack doesn't go completely quiet at night, especially in autumn. Every once in a while, the Canada geese get a panic attack, and a chorus of ill-tempered honking ensues. But mostly, it's the owls. In autumn, they make a pit stop in the woods beside the pond, serenading my nighttime barn chores and volleying their plaintiff songs back and forth from trees standing sentinel at the edges of my property. It's a reverberating, homey, hunkered-down sort of sound that always feels like eavesdropping on pillow talk. In winter, I might well be listening in on bedroom activities, because Ray explained that many owls nest in winter, timing the hatching of their young for when squirrels and rabbits also give birth. It's one of the cold realities of survival.

The parley between what takes flight and what scampers along the earth makes me infinitely grateful that I steward so many different habitats for creatures great and small. Being a way station or a meeting point for a flock on the move is sort of thrilling. It's a strong incentive for leaving a meadow undeveloped. It's also a cogent reason to preserve untouched the woods around a pond and the trees ringing a property. Ray explained that birds are especially fond of fallen tree stumps to supply insects and shelter when gearing up for migration or the colder weather ahead. It's just another instance when leaving it be sounds awfully good.

KEEPING THE GARDEN HUMMING

BIRDS ARE NOT the only squadrons happening in autumn. Watching the final work crews laboring like the dickens to bring in the last harvest can get me all misty. No, I'm not speaking of the last swipe of the lawnmowers. I'm referring to a much more subtle hum. There's something so touching about those diligent little bees, butterflies, flies, hummingbirds, and other working-class insects doing their last sorties of the season. They buzz around tirelessly milking the pre-frost nectar production for all it's worth, sometimes staging their final binge in preparation for migration, sometimes readying for a long winter's slumber. The least I can do is serve up the fodder.

I can certainly see why some gardens fizzle out in fall. After all, it's not a time of year when nurseries are heavily stocked with inventory luring you to make purchases. From the marketing point of view, fall is pretty much a forgotten season. Nurseries are winding down and putting inventory on sale, and beyond some mums and flowering cabbage, garden centers usually let the stock run down to nil. The typical retail nursery isn't bulking up on plants that perform in autumn. For ideas on what to grow for the late show, we're pretty much on our own. Not only are we left to our own devices, but acquiring likely candidates is also challenging in autumn. You would do well to plan ahead and buy autumn-performing plants in spring or early summer when garden centers are well stocked (or willing to special order), and plant them long before autumn arrives. Not only will acquisition be easier, but the plants will also stand a better chance of surviving through the winter.

Given that nurseries tend to leave you stranded, I suggest going on garden tours (the Garden Conservancy Open Days Program is a

wonderful resource for this endeavor) and jotting notes about what you find growing in gardens that feature an autumn-flowering crescendo. Purchase and plant the following spring, because many autumn bloomers prefer to be situated for many months prior to their fall display.

Then listen up, because autumn can be just as loud as any season—if not noisier. The bumblebees are especially diligent, but the frenzy from all pollinators hits a higher pitch. In my garden, all sorts of pollinators go bananas over the sedums and asters, and the garden is heavily stocked with those late-season performers specifically for the insects. Every type of

The meadow beside the goat pasture is billowing with goodies for pollinators in autumn.

sedum is installed, and I watch appreciatively as bees romance the flowers from bud stage onward. The gravelly, sun-baked lawn-alternative garden hosts the showy blue-flowering asters such as *Symphyotrichum oblongifolium* 'Raydon's Favorite' and 'October Skies'. Further afield, in the meadow, species asters romp, bolstered with *S. lateriflorum* 'Lady in Black' and other little nuggets that are hard to prune into shape. But sedums and asters are only part of the smorgasbord. The garden is studded with perennial agastaches, *Asclepias tuberosa*, heleniums, rudbeckias, echinaceas, cimicifuga, and phlox to keep the work crews humming. Buddlejas are a big part of the buffet, but I keep them scrupulously deadheaded to prevent seed set—a development that can lead to invasiveness issues.

Meanwhile, the meadow sounds like a factory in high production mode. This is really the meadow's moment in the sun, and it's been gathering girth and gearing toward autumn all year. My meadow is heavy on goldenrod, asters, milkweed, phlox, pycnanthemum, *Monarda fistulosa*, and Joe Pye weed—all of which thrill pollinators. I've encouraged the milkweed with monarchs in mind, letting it seed around the perimeter. On purpose, the meadow does not receive its annual shearing until the moment before snow is scheduled, just in case any seeds are still floating around. Basically, the goldenrod can be a bully, so I maintain diversity by inserting other players and encouraging them to self-seed.

In addition to the perennials in the garden and window boxes, late-season annuals provide a fountain of nectar for the little buzzers. I stuffed some *Celosia argentea* 'Intenz' into the window boxes as a stopgap measure after the hellebores had finally given up their season-long surge. The pollinators flocked. Even the hummingbirds paid a call. At one point a horde of sparrows noisily descended, giving Einstein an eyeful from his inside-the-window viewing station. Farther afield, the zinnias, tithonia, dahlias, marigolds, and *Verbena bonariensis* surrounding the vegetable beds bring up the drone of busy bugs purring away. The annuals actually started as a salute to my sense of sight, but my ears also caught wind of the benefits. And isn't that how this is supposed to work? Where one sense is served, other stimuli follow.

CRUNCH TIME

I F YOU EVER want to sneak up to my front door, it's best to avoid crunch time. Autumn is not the moment to stage any sort of stealth mission. There is no such thing as a furtive approach in fall. Any hope of clandestine access is squelched beneath your feet, and bursting on the scene is a physical impossibility. To penetrate my property from October to the first snow, you are going to wade through a sea of leaves, which entails a whole lot of shuffling, crackling, and crunching. And that's before I've raked. When I start organizing the downfall into piles, it's even worse—or better, from a home-security standpoint.

Autumn has its own singular buzz. As I write this, the whir of distant and not-so-distant leaf blowers echoes in the air. On the one hand, it disturbs the sweet chorus of natural autumn sounds in the countryside, breaking up the twittering of birds and vocalizing of goats urgently in heat (my Swiss-breed Saanens come into heat only in autumn, thank goodness). On the other hand, my neighbors' leaves will not be cluttering over to join the assemblage already populating my garden. Leaves like to cluster together. In particular, they like to meet beneath my microbiotas and chamaecyparises, neither of which appreciates their company. They get tangled up in the asters and snarled in the oregano—a sight that looks pretty for about one day before the fallen leaves turn from their radiant shades to crackling brown. Leaf blowers are not a totally unwelcome sound as long as they don't roar along on my property.

So I rake. Remember raking? Let me jiggle your long-term memory. Raking is the somewhat archaic practice of using a many-pronged long-handled device to move leaves from one place to another. It works this magic solely on the power of your biceps. Until you apply your rake to a pile of leaves, it makes no sound whatsoever. Think of a broom, and you're getting warm.

(FOLLOWING PAGES) Raking leaves gets tiresome, but it is also therapeutic and rhythmic.

I intend to be the last living nod toward this method of maneuvering fallen foliage from one place to another. Long after everyone else in the universe has bought blowers, I intend to keep right on raking. Snicker if you will, but I just don't see the point of blowing leaves over to the edge of the property just to have them hitch the first gust back to home base. I'll also take the satisfying shuffle, shuffle, shuffle, whoosh sound over the deafening whirr any day.

I do understand why the mow-and-blow crowd has such a fervent love affair with blowers. Blowers are dynamic. Beyond just moving leaves, they send plant parts, seedheads, and mulch racing around. They have the power, but it's just not the same. Show me the guy with a leaf blower in hand causing a whirlwind, and I'll defy him to identify any of the plants he just denuded. Blowing is a singularly blind sport that also entails ear protection. So that's several senses that don't benefit or are negatively impacted in your leaf-relocation endeavor.

You might say my affinity for rakes is just the sour grapes of a 90-pound weakling unable to pull a ripcord effectively. And you might be right. But there is something infinitely fulfilling about unearthing the herbaceous peony with its tawny blush leaves still intact and rejoicing because I will be enjoying its color for another few weeks. Granted, I want the ankle-deep drifts of immense, sickly gray catalpa leaves dispatched with as much haste as possible. But I also have a deep-rooted desire to hang on to the fragile puffs of clematis seeds as long as they will cling to the trellis near the tree's trunk. It's the difference between wanting summer gone now and dawdling over fond adieus. Plus, who doesn't love marveling over the colorful confetti of what was once summer as it's loaded onto the tarp?

For better or worse, I scratch away at the leaves every autumn, gathering them onto tarps and dragging them down to form a natural mulch in the woods with the goal of suppressing invasive plants. I corral them along the periphery of the property to surround the shrubs that mark my boundaries, thereby inhibiting weeds. I wish it was merely one weekend's pastime, but it goes on and on. Every evening, I'm out there scratching away. Every weekend, communing with the leaves figures into my social calendar. I brought this on myself, for sure. No trees resided on this property prior to my residence aside from a few gigantic and very senior sugar maples, a catalpa (which would easily win an award for Messiest Tree in the Universe because of those huge leaves that drop the morning after the first severe frost and its long, slender seedpods, which are a slippery safety hazard), a black walnut, and the spruces (which shed only pinecones). Leaves and the need for their redistribution is a fringe benefit of being a horticultural fanatic. As I said, the preponderance of leaves at Furthermore is my own doing.

I brandish the rake the moment the black walnut disrobes to remove its debris before the toxin-laden mess starts washing down to the berry garden. Then, whenever it isn't raining or windy (which doesn't leave many opportunities), from the first sugar maple leaf drop to the last magnolia and oak leaves, you'll find me wielding a rake and martialing tarps. This could easily rank as aerobic exercise. Constant, daily aerobic exercise.

Anyone who still rakes leaves will tell you that one of the perks is audible. I love to listen to the sound of leaves being shuffled around. Another perk goes to the juncos and tufted titmice that glory in the debris left behind in the gravel driveway (yet another advantage to gravel versus paving). They flit around, chipping happily at their newfound treasure, giddily gleaning any salvageable seeds. With a little planning, you might even be able to add the high-pitched glee of children jumping into the piles of leaves. But let's face it; after maneuvering about twenty huge tarploads of leaves, there is one sound that everyone is going to hear: the groan that accompanies a very weary back.

Touch

GET A GRIP

NUMBNESS IS NEVER a good thing in the garden, so here's another ode to gloves. At all times of year, gloves seem like a good way to protect your most valuable asset. I know—grimy, work-worn hands are a gardener's proof of authenticity. Flash some dirt-encrusted fingernails in somebody's direction, and that's living proof that you're out there doing hand-to-hand combat with the soil. Open any gardening magazine, and chances are you'll come upon a photo of someone's labor-etched hands fondling vegetables or grasping a bouquet of flowers. The image is compelling, I agree. But is it sustainable?

Unprotected fingers leave too much exposed. That's true at any time of year, but fall really drives home the need for gloves. When you add nippy weather to the list of hazards that your fingers are apt to encounter as the temperatures drop and fall cleanup ensues, the stakes are upped. Skip gloves right now, and you will be feeling the consequences for months to come.

Some women have an arsenal of shoes at their beck and call. A stack of gloves poised by the door is more my speed. The collection includes mud gloves, leather gloves, lined gloves, driving gloves, gauntlets, and wool gloves. If you think this has anything to do with making a fashion statement, take a look at the pile. It is about dressing for success because I select specifically for the job at hand.

Wear the wrong gloves in autumn, and your hands are going to suffer. Nothing calls a halt to progress faster than frigid fingers. You can get away with any old gloves while raking as long as they prevent blisters. But when you start getting down and intimate with cold, wet, icy garden debris, glove selection becomes critical. Atlas Super Grip or nitrile gloves are my handwear of choice for most gardening applications that require dexterity. But autumn adds another layer of urgency to glove demands. When

(FOLLOWING PAGE) During fall cleanup, wearing gloves is particularly critical.

the work gets icy, you have to protect fingers from more than just the standard bruises, rips, and tears that come with the job. They want to be warm.

Fingers can go numb only a couple of times before chilblains set in. If you have no idea what I'm talking about, lucky you. Southern gardeners are probably never exposed to this occupational health hazard. Chilblains are painful, red, irritated patches of itchy skin. Excessive chilblains look and feel like someone mangled your fingers. All sorts of creams are out there to cure them, but none is magic. The best solution is preventive action. West County gloves are fully equipped with silicone dots on the reinforced fingers for grabability, spandex mesh on the back, and brow wipes on the thumbs (who wants to remove gloves to wipe that brow?). My only beef is that the terry-cloth padding at the cuff tends to collect dirt, but they are fully washable. Later, as the weather gets colder, lined leather gloves (such as those offered by Womanswork) that fit properly are the way to go.

Bulky lined gloves get in the way of fast progress for delicate garden chores such as replanting and pruning, but waiting for your fingers to complain is a seriously bad idea. It's a coin toss between struggling to do intricate work wearing gloves and being able to endure working for extended periods of time thanks to the gloves. In autumn, when every minute is critical in the countdown, staying comfortable outside is golden.

UNDERGROUND ASSETS

I HAVE A conspiracy theory linking chiropractors to the autumn-planting bulb trend. For some reason, even though we've had a whole summer to get into shape preparing for this marathon, bulb planting is still hell on the musculoskeletal system. The problem probably lies in the magnitude of the endeavor, because bulbs are gregarious. There is no such thing as a singular bachelor bulb; they work only in communal situations. Plus, you have to factor in the pressure. This planting spree must occur during a narrow window of time that can end at a moment's notice without a whole lot of forewarning. We know all about long-range weather predictions and their massive margin of error. So we work diligently—every minute counts as the days shorten and the stacks of bulb crates do not diminish correspondingly. And then there's greed. Show me the gardeners who can limit themselves to just twenty-five tulips, and I'll send them a juicier catalog.

It all boils down to a lot of backbreaking labor in a brief amount of time. As in: many holes being dug in rapid succession, often drilled (sometimes literally) into places where no one has dug a hole before. I tuck my tulips into the same spot every year, so that's easy mining. But I forge into no-man's-land for the hyacinths and daffodils while trying to beautify far-flung spaces that desperately need a face-lift. In spring, they'll be a lifesaver. In spring, all the aching agony will be long forgotten in light of the color sweeping our world again. But before then, there is a calendar full of remedial doctor's appointments to get myself back in alignment.

Unfortunately, there is no easy fix. Bulb planting is arduous, and there is no silver bullet. All those bulb planters hawked in catalogs are largely useless—the more expensive the so-called labor-saving contraption is, the less functional it proves. Take the stand-up device with the long shaft, wide handle, and circular funnel for inserting bulbs in borders. In theory you won't have to bend over or bob up and down into a deep squat. You just dig in and drop the bulb from a standing position. Dream on: the device will inevitably hit obstructing stones or get clogged up. The funnel-shaped handheld devices are equally ill-conceived, although not as expensive. If only I could write a prescription for the perfect tool for planting bulbs painlessly and efficiently, preferably from an upright position.

Bulb planting is a particularly bouncy sport. As a remedy, try excavating chunks of space with a shovel and planting as many bulbs as possible side by side in a communal plot. This practice definitely saves your back. But the approach is rarely practicable in a perennial border

---

Hyacinth bulbs can cause a nasty dermatological reaction
in some people—wear gloves when handling.

setting, and many gardeners (including moi) are adopting the integrated approach wherein spring bulbs segue into late spring, summer, and autumn perennials that pick up the beat. In other words, bulbs are part of a much larger picture. That entails loads of individual holes. I've tried augers (especially where the soil is compacted) with some success. But I always seem to go back to a trowel. The Dutch are wedded to a trowel with a heart-shaped blade (and they know a thing or two about bulb planting), but the blade has no scoop indentation, so it works best in a prepared bed. I prefer a slender-bladed trowel with a pointed tip. With that weapon, you can wedge your bulbs into crevices between perennials. Be sure to find a sturdy model. There are special bulb trowels on the market specifically for the job, but any good trowel will do. You plunge the blade down to the target depth, pull the soil toward you, insert the bulb, and fill it in. This sounds streamlined, unless you're doing it 1,000 times. Then it gets dizzying.

Your back is not the only body part to complain. Hands take a beating. True, your paws had the entire season to toughen up. But there's something about the frigid weather, the cold stony soil, and the bulbs themselves that is hurtful. In particular, hyacinth bulbs contain calcium oxalate crystals (called raphides) that can cause a nasty dermatological reaction. Daffodils and tulips also have raphides, but not in such high quantities. The reaction manifests in many ways, but an itch is common (the condition can also occur when cutting daffodil stems). I'm not suggesting that you swear off bulbs (unless your reaction is particularly nettlesome), but always wear gloves when handling them. Plus, wash with cold water immediately after each bulb interaction. Seek medical advice if the situation worsens. And never touch or rub your eyes when working with bulbs.

Even though bulbs can bite, even though you have to grovel to do the job, and even though they always come in hordes (many bulb catalogs don't even give you the prudence option; they offer in quantity only), you need to plant bulbs. The backache is temporary and usually placated by a long soak in the bathtub (again, wash your hands first). Fingers take a while to heal. But by spring, all that pain is a thing of the past. What lingers is the elation that comes from the invigorating presence of an onslaught of flowers stampeding around your garden. That's worth a groan or two.

THORNY SUBJECTS

S OMETIMES CLEANUP brings out the worst in plants. While wrenching them from the soil, you're apt to reveal traits that slipped under the radar. I'm not saying that they brandish artillery in the futile attempt to withstand autumn cleanup intact, but sometimes it feels that way. What's actually happening is that you're suddenly in a close dialogue with stems, branches, and other meandering appendages that were pretty much on their own during the growing season. Running your fingers up and down stems can destroy the copacetic relationship you had with some of your favorite botanical buddies. Who knew that asparagus gone to seed had such nasty barbs? If you try cutting it down, its prickly personality becomes all too painfully apparent.

It's the intimacy that hurts. From a distance, thorns have a jagged beauty—if you see them at all. Every year I forget about the antisocial aspect of asparagus, and every year I am reminded. Of course, those cleomes, asparagus, and various rubus aren't really carrying concealed weapons; we just don't take time to study them until the snippers come out. Then all is revealed.

All sorts of plants get mean when removal is imminent. Underneath all those flouncy, colorful bracts, bougainvilleas are heavily barbed. And flowering quince (*Chaenomeles speciosa*) looks innocent until you grab a branch to start disciplinary action, attempting to shear it into a socialite from an ill-kempt ragamuffin. It always comes as a shock when trailing plants bite back. Try cleaning up beneath *Cotoneaster horizontalis* sometime, and its vicious side will be revealed. *Juniperus communis* doesn't have thorns, but it feels like it does. Whatever you want to call the scratch that juniper inflicts, it hurts nonetheless—and it gives many people a rash. No matter how handsome they might be, most raspberries have serious thorns. In fact, beware of anything with "bramble" in its name,

---

(FOLLOWING PAGES) Rugosa roses can bite when you try to prune them back.

like the gorgeous variegated ghost bramble (*Rubus cockburnianus* 'Razzle Dazzle') and neon yellow–leaved lemon lace bramble (*R. parvifolius* 'Lemon Lace'). Obviously, if "thorn" is part of a plant's common name, it's a dead giveaway that you should be cautious. The scratchy penchant of firethorns (*Pyracantha coccinea* and cultivars) and hawthorns (*Crataegus monogyna*) should come as no surprise. And if you don't realize that the hardy orange (*Poncirus trifoliata*) has daggers, you're just not looking. Japanese barberry (*Berberis thunbergii*) is a bad idea because of its invasive personality, so I have no sympathy when someone who plants it on purpose gets ripped. But for those of us who take autumn as prime invasive-diminishing season, ridding the property of Japanese barberry can be one of the season's most painful experiences.

Roses are the worst vines and shrubs to discipline. I leave them for last when cutting back, and sometimes I wait until late winter. I don't relish being shredded, but I also don't want them sending energy into sprouting if we get a late-season warming. And pruning seems to spark the sprout response in roses. Always go into the war of the roses armed with gauntlet gloves and as much padded clothing as possible. Wearing pretattered garments is a brilliant idea. For all these reasons, you might prefer the thornless 'Zéphirine Drouhin' climbing rose to keep the pruning process painless and avoid frisking visitors. Mercifully, David Austin Roses has bred some thornless or nearly thornless roses; check their website for 'Brother Cadfael', 'Tea Clipper', 'Lichfield Angel', 'James Galway', 'The Generous Gardener', 'Kew Gardens', 'A Shropshire Lad', 'Mortimer Sackler', 'Snow Goose', and 'Leander', among others.

Regular mud gloves and the like are not sufficient for working with roses. Instead, go for the padded leather editions (Womanswork makes some good-quality products) to protect your most precious tool from plants with tattering tendencies. Pitted against roses and many other thorny subjects, you might still come out with scratches on your face, shoulders, and legs. Becoming a blood brother (or sister) when groping around the garden is not easy to avoid. Look before you grasp. This counseling is apt for any aspect of life.

Taste

JUST PEACHY

A LOT OF lines have been blurred in these pages. For many subjects, it was difficult to choose the section where they would be discussed. But there was no question where peaches would fit, because my peaches will probably never win a beauty pageant. However, blemishes are totally superfluous when savoring your very own freshly plucked peaches with the juice dribbling decadently down your chin. When you are bound to pop your own ripe morsels of fruit into your mouth the moment they mature, who cares what they look like? The beauty of homegrown fruit is that it needs to show off for no one. The only qualification is that it is ready for harvest. Something about the nuances of flavor from your very own hard-earned harvest is incomparable. The fruit is never uniform. From a supermarket standpoint, maybe your peaches wouldn't compare favorably with the bins of cookie-cutter, picture-perfect peaches that they load on the shelf by the bushelful. But one taste, and you'll never again bother with the supermarket offerings.

Although I grow a swarm of different berries (honestly, there's standing room only in my berry patch), so far peaches are my sole stone fruit. A lone peach tree stands as the (slightly gawky) focal point in the center of the circular vegetable garden, satisfying all needs for fresh fruit. That one 'Reliance' peach efficiently produces bushels. If I start consuming the crop in late summer, I just might finish the last peach by frost. I bring them inside to ripen on windowsills and in the greenhouse (to thumb my nose at the squirrels); and morning, noon, and night, peaches equal sustenance. If it were possible to continue all year, I would gladly commit to the peach diet.

In the ease-of-cultivation category, 'Reliance' gets high marks. It suffers no issues (except perhaps peach borer, a foe that doesn't pester us here). It boasts a reliable harvest (except when a very late spring frost smites the

There is nothing like a ripe peach plucked straight from the tree.

flowers, and that's happened only twice). No spraying is necessary. And it tolerates my dorky pruning abilities. Peaches were the first non-native fruit introduced into this country; the Spaniards brought them to Florida. That's a testimony to their ease of cultivation. Unlike apples, which require an arsenal of stopgap measures to thwart all the problems to which they are prone, peaches are simple.

In zone 5, we are just a couple of zones too chilly to winter figs outdoors. A few years ago, I visited Phil Forsyth, director of the Philadelphia Orchard Project. Phil is a big fan of figs as the ideal urban fruit in zone 7. In Philadelphia, he can also plant 'Nikita's Gift' persimmon, paw paws, apricots, plums, serviceberries, Asian pears, 'Seckel' pears, as well as a so-called hardy fig. At one of his inner-city orchards, I sampled my first jujube (*Ziziphus jujuba*), a date-like, cherry-size, pop-in-your-mouth tasty sensation. If Phil has his way and Philadelphia's vacant lots are converted to orchards, the city will soon be savoring the harvest and expanding their culinary vistas.

Meanwhile, back at Furthermore, I'm thinking of extending the season with more peach varieties. 'Veteran' and 'Autumn Rose' are suggested for early-autumn eating. Rutgers recommends 'Encore', 'Gloria', 'Messina', 'Flamin' Fury', and 'Laurol' for late-season ripening. But it's hard to beat 'Reliance' for hardiness. The two years when my peach failed to produce a crop, it was nothing short of a tragedy. Even with their physical imperfections, peaches are juicy, nectar-filled decadence. You owe it to your mouth to indulge.

CARROT GOLD

A UTUMN IS THAT rare interlude when cooking traditions and crops finally coincide. When it's prime time for carrots, beets, and the like, everyone is digging through their stir-fry root crop recipes for holiday fare. If it weren't for my carrot crop, I wouldn't know what to bring to

Thanksgiving dinner. Years ago, I found a recipe for stir-fry carrots with caraway seeds, and it's probably the only reason I get invited back to the annual family feast.

I was not a huge carrot fan until I read Eliot Coleman enthuse on the subject of winter carrots. Around here, in Voleland, winter carrots are an unattainable luxury. It would be like setting up underground vole-feeding stations where those despicable varmints could do their subterranean dining without fear of being disturbed. I must harvest the carrots on or before Thanksgiving in order to enjoy the crop without the nibble marks from nasty little critters with disgusting table manners and piggish eating habits.

In my experience, carrots aren't a vole's first line of attack—that award goes to the sweet potatoes. You are safe leaving carrots in the ground until November. Meanwhile, as Eliot informed us, carrots spend cold weather converting their starches to sugars. That explains why a carrot in mid-summer is okay in a pinch, but a carrot in autumn almost qualifies as a dessert item. Eliot calls them candy carrots, and one bite will make a believer out of you. In warm weather, carrots need a little jazzing up with dressing, sauces, raisins, or walnuts. In autumn, they stand on their own as raw finger food.

I used to grow half an acre of carrots annually. At the time, we were all serious carrot-juice addicts. We stored crates of carrots in the root cellar, and they got us through the winter. So I'm pretty well versed on the whole sequence of sowing, thinning, and hoeing carrots. I did them in long rows, and every friend who stopped by during summer break was enlisted to crawl down a row and pluck when thinning time rolled around. Friends knew to bring shorts rather than ruin the knees of a good pair of jeans. To say that it was labor intensive is an understatement.

For many reasons (including economics and lack of a juicer), I no longer do carrots wholesale. Nowadays, a row pretty much satisfies my appetite. Every year, I order early- and later-season carrots, but I rarely have success with the second sowing because of midsummer droughts

---

(FOLLOWING PAGE) Sow carrot seeds in late summer or very early autumn, and you can squeeze in a crop for storage.

that have been the rule recently. On the off year when we aren't mired in a drought, a thunderstorm deluge washes out the tiny seeds or the equally untenacious seedlings. No matter: one row of 'Nelson' carrots does the job. 'Nelson' is a plump, stubby variety that plunges down 5 to 6 inches and is easy to dig because the roots don't taper off. It is predictable, delicious, and as sweet as honey in autumn. I don't care that it's not uniform.

In the newest-and-latest department, multicolored carrots are all the rage. In my experience, carrots that are colors other than orange are generally pithy beyond baby carrot stage. That trait will probably change with time and good breeding. As far as other root crops are concerned, parsnips completely elude my prowess (sadly, because I seriously adore them). Beets, another favorite, are such tempting fare for voles that they fall victim as soon as the roots start to swell. Celeriac is a long-season root crop that requires some planning, but it's worth the space if you like sweet tender root vegetables. And, finally, rutabagas. Not even the goats will consume rutabagas in any way, shape, or form—and that's saying something. So that leaves the carrots, which are now stored in my refrigerator for lack of a root cellar. But that's if I have any left over after I prepare my Thanksgiving dish.

CABBAGES AND KINGS

F ROST IS CRUEL punishment for vegetables. In fact, it's usually lethal. In its take-no-prisoners approach, frost smites some of the choicest delicacies, like the eggplant, celery, and basil. But as the temperatures drop, cabbages and other members of the cole clan add succulent nuances in flavor. If linking broccoli with savory sounds like an oxymoron to you, keep reading.

Say what you will about kale (and my friends on social media have plenty of opinions, none complimentary), the taste improves dramatically after frost. I agree that during the summer months, kale has a long way to go before reaching savory status. But after a few snappy frosts, the new growth becomes tender, juicy, and mildly flavorful in a less chewy way than its summer metamorphosis. I've found a few kales that stand a really good chance of silencing your gag response. As a midsummer lettuce substitute, I tried the ultra-frilly kale varieties from Fruition Seeds, 'Bear Necessities' being a favorite and 'Siber Frill' employed as a tickle-as-it-goes-down garnish that I didn't take too seriously. After frost, I got serious. Come autumn, when other veggie staples are bowing out and kale moves into a sustenance-level slot, 'Redbor' and 'Red Russian' step up to the plate. From the first frost onward, they stop tasting like something the doctor ordered.

But the real transformational magic happens with Brussels sprouts. Talk about a vegetable that goes from verging-on-inedible to melt-in-your-mouth-I-can't-get-enough. Brussels sprouts give the cabbage family a good name. After dabbling in a whole lot of Brussels sprouts over the years, there have been moments when I was tempted to give up because of low yield of tiny nubbins not worth the space they monopolized ('Diablo', this means you). Brussels sprouts are hefty plants. They stand about a yard or taller in height with plenty of leaves until late summer, when they begin dropping leaves with embarrassing frequency. Because I have faith and because tasting other people's Brussels sprouts made a believer out of me, I kept on experimenting. 'Hestia' changed my relationship with Brussels sprouts for the better. It is relatively short and the sprouts are generous in size. But don't assess performance on produce before frost. Even then, give Brussels sprouts until Thanksgiving to really prove its stuff. The plant stops adding height and sheds lower leaves, but the sprouts keep on developing throughout autumn. In fact, you can usually shovel your way into the garden and harvest some Brussels sprouts after a snowstorm. But don't wait too long. Eventually, after being frozen and thawed repeatedly, they go over the brink. When you finally fetch them indoors, they fail to store successfully for more than a day in the refrigerator. That observation is based on sadder-but-wiser procrastination.

Succession-planted 'Blue Meadow' broccoli keeps
the table stocked with a favorite vegetable.

Cabbages operate along the exact same lines. I don't even bother giving my cabbages a passing pat on the head until late in the season. As autumn arrives, they begin to attain maturity. Again, it's a fine line between the optimal harvest moment and when they become overly ripe and develop fissures that rival the San Andreas Fault. Cabbages have the potential to become big, handsome hunks, so feel free to select the best-looking varieties. Current personal darlings are 'Deadon' (a Savoy) and 'Ruby Perfection' for purple varieties, and 'Caraflex' because cone-shaped cabbage heads are just plain fun. They all improve after a nip of frost.

For me, cauliflower is wishful thinking. But to date, my hands-down favorite vegetable has eluded me. Every year I experiment with a different cauliflower in the vain hope that my soul mate is out there. At best, these attempts have produced only spindly heads that rot rapidly. I'm working on it.

Basically, there isn't a cole crop that I won't eagerly gobble (well, maybe collards are pushing it). In spring, I jump on the kohlrabi with a fork and knife as soon as the stems begin to swell. Kohlrabi turns pithy when temperatures start to heat up (even purple 'Kolibri', famed for retaining its tenderness, eventually goes south), and late crops don't fare so well.

Best of all is broccoli. Those tender little florets are sustenance. You can grow succession crops of broccoli throughout the summer and into fall, when head production slows but doesn't cease. My favorites are 'Bay Meadows' and 'Arcadia'. After the initial harvest, coax a second crop of side shoots and then give the spot over to the next generation and sow more broccoli. This might sound like slow torture to your kids, but someday they'll love you for it.

So here's the theory: folks who make ugly faces at any reference to a cole crop just haven't waited long enough. Be patient with your Brussels sprouts and don't make snap judgments about your kale. Their time will come.

THE LATE SHOW

Y OU'VE SOWN and reaped. You've harvested some late arrivals that took the entire growing season to mature. And maybe you're weary. Perhaps you are pretty much ready to throw in the trowel and call it quits for the year. Don't. Instead, summon another ounce of energy and push your garden to its limits. Your tummy will thank you. Play your cards right, and it's possible to sneak in another season of salad greens.

Just like everyone else, I begin to peter out by September. Although a brisk succession of vegetables is kept pumping through most of summer, sometimes the routine falls apart late in the year. And that leaves nothing but the grocery store to feed my hunger for greens. After eating your own produce for several months, supermarket fare is seriously blah. Whether it's because you've been toiling over those little plants for weeks or because of the seasoning dripping from your sweaty brow, homegrown food just tastes better. If you have one iota of energy left, invest it in a late crop. You won't be sorry.

Hit the raised beds not much later than the first of September. Finding space is not usually an issue—you probably have empty lettuce rows that bolted in the heat of summer. Other crops have probably been harvested and created space. Back when I was growing sweet potatoes (before the voles sent out an all-points bulletin announcing that fact), an entire raised bed of sweet potatoes left room to sneak in one more relay of vegetables. Here's the plan: buy some compost (you can usually get it for a song in autumn), spread it on and hoe it in, and go to work with some seed packets. The trick lies in finding short-season greens to bring your scheme to life.

I live on lettuce, so that's my mainstay. For autumn, try 'Gentilina', 'Optima', and 'Adriana'. When cold weather (as opposed to merely chilly) is forecast, gobble down lettuces in their youth—autumn is all about grabbing the goodies while they still exist. You might also grow spinach ('Butterflay' does beautifully at this time of year) and put in another crop of Swiss chard ('Bright Lights' is the most fun, although 'Fordhook

Giant' is faster and seems to be more productive). Note that buttery, tender Swiss chard in autumn is a whole different taste sensation than its earlier incarnation.

Warning: mothering might be necessary when you first plant your autumn crops. In early September, you could still be on the tailwind of August's hot, dry tendencies. Water the seeds in when sowing, and keep watering until they germinate. By that time, autumn's cooler weather should be in full swing, and if you say your prayers every night, autumn rains might be sprinkling down. While saying those prayers, please insert a special request for rain of the gentle genre. Deluges are counterproductive.

Your strategy might work, or an early frost might turn your efforts into mush. But at least you tried to extend the season and give the grocery store's produce department the cold shoulder. And what do you have to lose? Maybe a few dollars for a seed packet. The compost is a good investment whenever you dish it out. Give it your best shot. Keep the momentum going. You can rest your weary self in winter.

'Bright Lights' Swiss chard tastes even more buttery after frost.

Winter

✳

Here comes the acid test. If you can fully plug in during winter, then you are well on your way to forging forward into the wild blue yonder. If you can make this season—when we usually bide our time, twiddle our green thumbs, and wait for easier deep digging—into a juncture that is totally, wholly, unabashedly, dynamically sensational, then you are on the road to filling in all the colors, smells, tastes, sounds, and feelings of your surroundings for the rest of your life.

The garden might be buried, but it still has a strong presence.

DID I SAY winter is the test? When else do you swing from abject boredom to fight-for-survival mode in a few brief hours? When else are you called to action from cabin fever to snow-shovel overdose between sunset and sunrise? When else do you wonder if you'll ever again see the sun rise or cast your eyes on the naked earth? This is when the elements unleash their fury. And this is when you have time to really savor what is going on. Winter could be an interlude when you dream about more profuse seasons, or winter can be just as sensually suffused as any other time.

The elements are howling, tingling, rushing, and they come out punching. They put you on the defensive. Sometimes you struggle to search for a muse that speaks on a positive note in winter. Sometimes you have to look inward. But real gardeners don't hibernate in winter: they just draw the focus closer around them. There is so much going on where you live, right at your elbow, sharing your home. And if not, you need to make it happen. If you don't, you're missing a huge opportunity to bond with nature. Winter can be fierce, but the counterpoint between the events outside and the beauty that you nurture close by is an awakening on a particularly dynamic level. Winter gives you the time to really practice all the skills you honed during gentler times.

So here you go. No green-thumb twiddling allowed. Eyes wide open; all your senses tuned in—check winter out, because a whole lot lies in store for those who perceive. You're not at the finish line. This is just the beginning.

Sight

SPARKLE

WINTER SPARKLES. People talk about the dazzle of summer, but this is a different sort of richness. You have to look for the wealth of winter, but it does exist. Go outside in winter, and it's as though someone tossed a king's ransom of diamonds at your feet. It's magic.

Every evening, my flashlight guides the journey between the back door and the goat barn. It could be just another chore under the cover of night. It could just be relays with water buckets. But the path is paved with bling. All you need is some heavy, hoary frost, and everything within eyeshot is phosphorescent. By moonlight, the twinkle is like a disco ball. Even the stray beams of the outdoor patio light evoke a thoroughly pleasant shimmer of scintillation. Add some sunrays and the phenomenon is turned up several notches. At a time of year when excitement of any sort is sparse, the glitz on the ground is big. With a little sugar frosting on the branches, you've got a William Turner.

If frost is bling, then snow is dazzling multiplied by infinity. If someone tossed all the jewels on Earth at your feet, it wouldn't compare to the wealth of a snowy field stretched as far as your eye can see. But that's not snow's only function. It also masks a multitude of sins. Camouflaging all the tasks left undone, secreting all the eyesores that haven't migrated to the top of your to-do list (the broken wheelbarrow in need of repair, the tumbled-down bench), snow is a procrastinating gardener's best friend. In fact, snow's complicity as a blanketing agent is our Plan B: "Should I drag all the eyesore bags of potting soil into the basement? No, why court possible back injury—they'll be covered in snow by the end of the week." But snow does more than just serve as a cover-up; it is also instructional.

Snow outlines the shape of the land. In other seasons, our eyes are diverted, flitting between flower beds, focusing on target destinations. When winter serves up a little sugar coating, it's all about the flow of form. Suddenly, the contours of the land are manifest in all their voluptuous rolls and discreet dips. When the lay of the land is cloaked in white, you can just sit back and celebrate it. The place feels so much more refined

when the stubble of the field is smoothed in white and the compost pile is a dollop with icing. You're not thinking about whether you'll be wheeling a heavy load up- or downhill; you're not judging or calculating. You are simply appreciating the lines. Who knew that the field swelled beyond the goat barn? Who realized that the meadow sent a gentle curve to dip ever so slightly into the lawn? You can use that knowledge when adorning your land. Or you can rest on your snow shovel for a few minutes, catch your breath, and simply notice the silhouette. Snow smooths out distractions; it does the land proud. Revel in its form.

Crystals make branches into treasures.

TELLTALE SIGNS

G RAND CENTRAL TERMINAL has nothing on my backyard. And who knew? Maybe an inch of snow fell last night; maybe less. But it was so revealing. Apparently, my backyard is a major travel hub. Unbeknownst to me (until this morning's revelation), a huge social gathering occurs every evening, if the tracks are to be trusted. Creatures come; creatures go; they hold line dances. They boogie all night, from the looks of it. And I'm not invited.

I would be the party pooper, of course. Oh, I wouldn't mind a bunny or two meeting clandestinely in the night. But if the tracks are to be trusted, dozens of rabbits are scampering incessantly back and forth. The tracks look like a map of New York City suburbs. Judging from the telltale signs, they crisscross frenetically all night long. And none of the attendees would be on my A list for invitations. In fact, I'm thinking of hiring bouncers.

Beyond the population explosion of my two most nefarious foes, deer and rabbits (and what the tracks do not reveal is what's going on underground), there seem to be a few crows scratching around. A lone opossum waddles in to poke around aimlessly by moonlight. An overweight raccoon checks the compost for anything appetizing. I can live with an opossum and a bachelor raccoon. It's the bunny boom that has me newly on guard.

You can foresee a lot of issues by checking the tracks. By heeding footprints, you can plan out your battle strategies and rally your forces. Granted, there's something poignant about tracks in the snow. When the temperatures have recently dipped into the single digits, it's consoling to see that life has survived. A single set of rabbit prints is a welcome sight, I suppose. But a convention center? Maybe not.

Note to self: fortify the vegetable garden gates with reinforced mesh fencing.

Evidence that wild turkeys were here.

THE SHAPE OF THINGS

I SHOULD HAVE pruned back the hydrangea. I see it clearly now, in all its gawky, disheveled, asymmetric glory. The same snow that disclosed the deer population also divulges artistic talent for shaping shrubs and trees. A few hours with the pruning shears before the snow impeded intimate contact, and that shrub would be my pride and joy. It's not an eyesore, to be certain. But it sure isn't a vision of splendor.

The wisest time investment you can make in winter is to prune everything within sight at its onset while you can still make contact. Shaping the shrubs and trees within your line of vision from the house or street will lead to many moments of contented contemplation. There are exceptions. My friends the Nichols brothers at MrMaple.com warn against Japanese maple pruning until mid- to late March. And we leave the buddlejas and caryopteris alone until they begin to sprout growth in spring. But you can whack at hydrangeas and shrubs of similar ilk whenever there is bare ground in winter. Start trimming in its youth, when a shrub is in its formative stages, and that plant's potential to achieve runway model status is multiplied. Granted, some trees were born with good bones, just like some gals have beauty-queen prospects. But many ugly ducklings can be sculpted into swans—it just might require a bit of extra work.

Someone in my town is incredibly adept with pruners. I see the signature handiwork glorifying the tennis court and flanking the town hall. Subjects that you wouldn't normally associate with fine physiques—like flowering quince, viburnums, and euonymus—are rendered into svelte figures that would grace the horticultural version of Hollywood, if the film industry ever decided to skew its sensibilities in a natural direction. Plants that are usually all arms and legs have been shorn into smooth round orbs with perfectly spaced branches bristling around their contours. You want to go up and pat their lines. They are ravishing in full flower in spring. But they are even more remarkable in winter, when you can see their interior network. Their coiffures probably took many generations of sculpting.

Your shrubs and trees could be equally impressive. Get out the shears and saws and hack away. Stand back and assess the plant's lines and start

guiding its progress. If you train early rather than try to nip and tuck later in life, you can create a superstar. Not all plants have the potential. For example, sumac seems to elude everyone's ability to whip it into shape. But even a forsythia can be a boasting point. In my town, the phantom pruner worked wonders with an unlikely rose of Sharon.

Of course, this feat is so critical in winter because anything bare-naked needs to be buff. Flaccid plants are bad in summer, but they're even more of a letdown in winter. Silhouetted against snow, they are outrageously divine—or not. Add the etching of snow running along their sinuous

A few extra swipes at the flowering cherry in early winter accents its physique.

muscles and be still my heart. But fitness training doesn't happen by accident. So gather your courage and get out there with your pruners. Tell that plant where to go. A couple of years ago, crippling cold caused all the smoke trees (*Cotinus coggygria*) in the neighborhood to die back to the snow line, which was about 3 feet. We all sucked in our breath, chopped off the dead wood, and prayed. Best summer ever for smoke trees. Everyone was walking around with chests puffed out in pride. You can have that feeling of accomplishment without the near-death experience. All it takes is shears and guts.

WINDOWSILL DRESSING

JACK FROST DOES his best artwork on my bedroom window. I wake up and don't even need to consult the thermometer outside. It's clear that the temperatures are in the single digits or below. Actually, it isn't clear at all—it's opaque. And that's when leaves really step out.

Here is yet another instance to plead for houseplants. Yes, the webs of crystals and etchings on the windows are masterful and breathtakingly riveting. They are your personal ever-changing monochromatic kaleidoscope—and they're free. But couple nature's illuminated brushstrokes on glass with some houseplants and maybe a few forcing vases, and you can skip the trip to the art museum and just stay home. Snowbound never looked so good.

Many perks are inherent in windowsill gardening. You enjoy stimuli up close, with an intimacy that is rarely experienced outdoors. But winter is a special case. The logistics of winter make it difficult or impossible to view the show outdoors for more than brief forays, whereas you can savor

---

With its stained glass–like leaves, *Begonia* 'Cathedral' cuts an especially fine figure silhouetted against the windowpanes.

what happens indoors at your leisure. And discovering the intricacies and patterns of tropical leaves is a big part of what winter has to offer. The ideal viewing system is backlit against frosty panes. If you thought seeing slides in a lecture was the perfect format, wait until you start coupling leaves against windowpanes. They are thrilling.

I'm prejudiced. Having worked with begonias most of my life, I am prone to pin any virtue on them. But try it. Begonia leaves attain another level of artistry silhouetted against frosty glass. The way light moves through the star-shaped leaves of *Begonia* 'Little Brother Montgomery' or even the common pond lily begonia, 'Erythrophylla', is eloquent to the utmost. Take that dialogue one step further and grow 'Cathedral', which has a stained glass–like leaf with built-in transparent wedges that allow light to pass through partially. That is the zenith of the begonia-light experience for leaf definition. But also take a look at the flowers. Begonia blossoms sparkle. Each flower is made up of crystals that capture and bounce light like hundreds of shining mirrors. Don't take my word for it. Buy one and behold.

Begonias are just the beginning. The pigments in many leaves become more pronounced when backlit, and winter is the best time to check it out. Bromeliads are particularly poignant. The light flowing through the leaf of a vriesea or neoregelia reveals seductive truths. When leaves are ultra-thin, the light play is spectacular. The sunbeams rushing through colorful iresine leaves rival a psychedelic lightshow.

Other flowers also do the bling thing. Hyacinth blossoms are among my favorites for that purpose, but the petals of forced tulips and daffodils run a close second. If those spring bulbs aren't usually defined as houseplants, you need to change the classification system. Any plant you want to adopt can be a houseplant.

But it's not just about light shining through leaves. Silhouettes are equally articulate. Stage an echeveria in front of that frosty windowpane and its gracefully arching flower stalks attain another level of poetry. The matte blue colors become more striking. Later in the day, if the sun falls on the window, melting the frost to speckled droplets of water, it's a whole different state of affairs. In winter, the frost gives you a reason to wake up—and stay riveted.

Smell

❋

COLD HARD FACTS

WINTER IS UNDER WAY outside with a vengeance. It's –15°F out there and that's teeth-chattering, knee-knocking, finger-numbing, skin-lashingly cold. If you don't know what I'm talking about, consider yourself extremely fortunate. Because at –15°F, sane people don't go outdoors. Our first selectman keeps volleying robocalls begging us to remain inside. But the goats are out in the barn, and I'm their support team. So out I go.

At frigid temperatures, smell comes in microbursts. First of all, your face is swathed in mufflers. But even through that filter, you feel the stinging sensation of the cold. So you are suddenly made aware of your nose beyond its usual daily function. It is that stinging protuberance in the center of your face. There's nothing like intense cold to turn your olfactory consciousness up a few notches.

Winter has a sharp scent. It smells like ice. The rushing air is the essence of pure unadulterated wind even before you start adding the many layers that wind bears on its back. That sharpness is the initial perception on the path to the goat barn. Upon arrival, the goat barn holds its own bouquet. When I lean over to grab a water bucket, whiffs of smell breach the scarf barricades. Anything organic has its sensual signature. My eyes are focusing on whatever the flashlight is illuminating. My hands are fumbling for latches, bucket handles, and hay bales. I reach out a mittened hand to deliver an encouraging pet to the thick, lush coats of the critters waiting for rations.

The hay—if it's good hay—greets me with a unique combination (every bale is different) of timothy, clover, and alfalfa. If there is any hint of mustiness, that bale is rejected. When the flashlight cannot possibly deliver information you need to make critical choices, your nose kicks in.

Through my mufflers, I catch whiffs of the goats, their hay,
and their rumen—the essence of winter.

Sweet fern in the center of a bale smells blissful, but the goats will refuse it. You smell your way to being a good shepherd.

At –15°F, the goats will, I hope, be chewing their cud furiously and, as they stretch their noses to identify who is beneath all those layers, I smell their strong, sour rumen. All the manure they continually produce to fertilize the garden sends out a top note beyond the smells of hay, grain, and the piping hot water. That manure will someday be the compost beneath the hydrangeas I'm planting next spring, so it's the smell of promise. As I trudge back up to the house, the neighbor's woodstove sends smoke signals as my layers of clothing flap open and shut with each footfall. Despite the fact that it's seriously buttoned down, winter has its smells.

Maybe the goat-barn scenario is not a universal experience, but every property has its correlations. When you walk your dog, when you fill the bird feeder, while you shovel the walkway for the postal carrier, as you fish in the snow for the newspaper or take the garbage to the curb, smell your path. Before I consciously collaborated with my senses, I had no idea how much I knew about my barn. A head cold first clued me in to the wealth of knowledge I gathered through my nose. After being deprived of that method of input for a week or so, the sudden rush of cognitive data was telling and invigorating. Suddenly, my route to the barn was more than just the twice-daily trudge. Now the experience has added another dimension to its fingerprint. So does rummaging through the pot pile to find just the right container and scooping the soil from the bin. Yes, there's the auditory racket. But they send out smell signals as well. I like to think that I can identify where I am in the dark by pungency. In winter, what better game to play?

BREATHING IN

T HERE'S NOTHING BETTER than coming home. I trudge up the front
walk burdened with the baggage of whatever was in the car, I stomp
off the snow and ice on the doormat. I push open the door (which always
sticks, but that's a different story), and I encounter Einstein crouched in
greeting beside it (or maybe he sat vigil for the last six hours—I'll never
know). A whoosh of cold air accompanies my entry, and the skirmish
begins. The warm, humid atmosphere in the entry corridor greenhouse
pounces on the puff of frigid fumes. They tussle in a territorial battle
before the home team eventually wins. By the time I've unwound my
scarf, everything has settled. I breathe in, and the perfume of home has
won me over.

Every house has its own scent, be it the smell of cleaning fluids and
carpeting or the fumes of a furnace pouring out the heat. Sometimes it's
mothballs emanating from the spare bedroom, occasionally it's wet dog.
Often, the atmosphere is thick with eau de warm dinner rolls or coffee
percolating from the kitchen. Although perfumers claim that freshly
baked bread is the universal favorite for scents, my aromatic taste takes
a different direction. I would rather rely on smells that pour out continually and require less kneading. I go for green essences.

When you garden indoors, the plants subtly inform the house's
breath. It won't be like the baritone vocalizing; it's not even a whisper.
It's more of a hum. But the symphony is always in flux. Plant-based
smells are forever changing. Some flower opens, some flower closes, it
mixes with the smell of cauliflower from the kitchen stove or the lemon
furniture polish. The balance alters with the light. It's different from
morning to afternoon, from daylight to evening, and from sunny conditions to cloudy days. When you water, the damp, warm smells have a
certain resonance compared to when the sun beats down on a lot of dry
soil. When plants are thirsty, their essential oils are different than when
they are hydrated. Brush the lavender or plectranthus with your elbow
while watering, rustle the leaves while washing the floors, and a puff of

perfume flows out to acknowledge the intimacy. Tickle the mint with your fingertips, and it laughs in scent bursts.

Flowers are more social than leaf aromas. Some wait for your nose to come into their general vicinity before revealing their aromatic identity, while others reach out to make a statement. When the citrus is flowering, it rushes out to grab you at the door. Sweet olive throws its fragrance across the room. Freesia fills a room with its high note; jasmine hangs heavily on the air. Angel's trumpets and night-blooming cereus spew out their scents, but only after dark. Orchids can be discreet or garrulous, but when the chocolate orchid opens, it reaches out to grab converts. No one is safe.

Every home has its own scent; every day is different. Whether it's a conscious effort or happenstance, you brew your own essence and it says a lot about who you are in relation to nature. If you just like green, or flowers are a high priority, those choices are manifest in your home's exhale. But the beauty of botanical breath is that it tends to flow together. In midwinter, mine is the heady elixir of citrus, the cinnamon-laced scent of pinwheel jasmine (*Trachelospermum asiaticum*), forced narcissus, hyacinth, and sometimes a hoya or two. Granted, the hyacinths might seem overpowering when you touch your nose to their flower spires, but dispersed over the whole room, they don't come off as exhibitionists. If I've hit the supermarket on the right day, the high note of a freesia in a vase mingles with the jasmine to create a thoroughly sublime tang that changes depending on the time of day and where I'm standing. Natural scents have definite advantages over man-made ones. Everything harmonizes.

When the sun pulsates through the window in summer, the intensity of its beams can bruise the little flasks that hold essential oils on leaf surfaces of herbs. That's no problem for the plant, which repairs the damage continually. And meanwhile, our noses benefit as the stronger scent is released into the air. Then the closed house (and airtight is the goal in winter) serves like a perfume bottle, corking up scents. Winter is prime time for natural, in-house scent brewing. That said, we count the nanoseconds until we can throw open the window and allow the smell of the great outdoors to waft in.

Slightly musky, definitely apt to send its scent wandering around, winter-blooming jasmine (*Jasminum polyanthum*) is one of winter's signature top notes.

❋

FREESIAS

F OR YOUR SENSE of smell, winter mostly unfolds indoors. Not many noses look forward to winter, but mine does. I spend the rest of the year anticipating the season when it can partake in the inimitable elixir of freesias. Try though I might, I can't quite recollect the exact scent of freesias off-season. I know it's sensational. I know that it's some sort of sublime combination of vanilla and high-pitched sweet candy (toss in a pinch of cinnamon, maybe), but beyond that, the olfactory memory refuses to be called up. When winter arrives, providing the first opportunity to apply nose to a freesia flower, it all comes flooding back. "Of course, that's the essence of freesia," you say to yourself, and try to store the scent for future reference in times of freesia famine.

I haven't gotten the hang of storing freesia corms from year to year, so there's always the pressure to hunt down freesias. Actually, that's not a difficult mission—just stalk the supermarket florist section. As Valentine's Day approaches, the freesias appear on display. Any freesia makes a graceful statement of arching stems that would compete favorably with a performance of *Swan Lake*. The trumpet-shaped flowers line the flower stems, each opening at its appointed moment, holding that ballet-like stance for several days to coincide with its fellows. They're all gorgeous. But not all freesias are created equal from an olfactory standpoint. Some have peppery scents that many nostrils find deeply disappointing. Some require plugging in your imagination to detect only the slightest tease of an aroma. Don't settle for anything less than full-blown bliss.

The white hybrids are most apt to send your nose into orbit. Single white 'Ambiance' dispatches your sense of smell to heaven and back. Blue 'Mercurius' is almost equally divine. The single pink 'Aleide' with a hint of yellow isn't as robust a scent, but it's a beautiful flower. Yellows ('Aladdin'

Hands down, the most intoxicating scent floats from the
pearly white throats of *Freesia* 'Ambiance'.

being a good one) are usually strongly scented. Double-flowered versions tend to be less endowed in the aroma department compared to their single kin. Why do they vary so markedly? Perhaps because of the parentage. Freesia cultivars have a complicated bloodline comprising several species. Some are lightly scented, while others will curl your toes.

Purchase freesias as cut flowers or buy them as potted plants. I indulge in both because winter is long and I'm a hedonist. The cuts usually appear on the market before potted plants make their debut, but potted freesias have a slow, seductive drama that lasts longer. With luck (and as much sunlight as you can muster), more buds will form beyond the initial presentation that you bought into at the store. Like most plants snagged at the supermarket, freesias are usually sold in pitiful, sandy soil. Transplant them to a handsomer presentation as soon as possible, but don't graduate them into a larger pot size, as freesias prefer good drainage. If you repot them in your own rich soil, watch your watering and let them dry out between drinks; the corms dislike soggy situations. Even if you don't meet most of these preferences, a freesia will probably continue along its path to open up buds developed prior to shipping to the supermarket. But treating them well encourages more flower stalks (and an elevated sense of personal achievement). You can prolong the ecstasy. Even winter has its highlights.

HYACINTHS

HYACINTHS ARE THE floozies on the windowsill. Rather than mincing words, why don't we just tell it straight? Hyacinths are tarts. I have yet to find a hyacinth with a subtle bone in its body. They are all brash, loud, garrulous party animals wearing flouncy tricked-out outfits and sending forth flirtatious scents that we might find slightly offensive—if it weren't midwinter. Right now, hyacinths are heaven. You cannot stroll past a hyacinth without being pulled in to its petals.

The hybrid hyacinths don't dwell in my garden outdoors. Instead, the nearly wild versions (multiflora types such as 'Festival' and 'Anastasia') hold sway come spring. Granted, they don't have the fat, foxtail-like plumes that have won *Hyacinthus orientalis* hybrids their standing ovations. But the lollipop-like flowers of the tricked-out hybrids wouldn't sync with the nearly wild mood of my yard. That's not to say I don't worship the plump hybrids in their spectrum of racy shades at the right interlude. I couldn't survive winter without them. I have tried to go on hyacinth detox, and ended up rushing to the supermarket, desperate for my January fix of forced hyacinths. Winter has its own set of rules.

So bring on the ooh-la-la colors. Hit us again with the knockout scents that might be more apropos in a bordello. In winter, you crave their brand of outlandish behavior. In fact, it can't come on quickly enough. Early winter is spent anticipating the hyacinth's signature brand of heady overkill. Countless moments are wasted checking the full array of forcing vases, monitoring for any sign of sprouting.

To prepare for that juncture, order bulbs early. You don't want to have a heartbreaking out-of-stock experience. Whisk the bulbs into the refrigerator upon arrival. At that point, they might as well remain in their shipping bags if the refrigerator does double duty as a food-storage unit. When a spare moment presents itself during the Thanksgiving weekend, pop those bulbs into forcing vases to line the windowsills. I'm downplaying that ritual, which is a fetish at Furthermore. The full arsenal of forcing vases (which somehow increases annually—I suspect they mate and produce offspring) is lined up by the sink and assigned matching or complementary hyacinths. Fashionistas pass less time sorting out their wardrobes than I spend accessorizing hyacinths. Each vase is filled to its cinched waist (neck, actually) with water, and a bulb is suspended just above the water line in the throat. Then they line the windowsills in anticipation.

Of course, hyacinths could sit pretty in pots, planted in soil. But conclusive tests have shown that you can fit more forcing vases than pots on a windowsill, and whoever has the most hyacinths wins. Don't believe those photos in catalogs showing a rainbow of forced hyacinths performing in unison. Hyacinths never blossom simultaneously. Planted on the same date, 'Miss Saigon' can be in full flower while 'Fairy White' isn't showing the slightest sign of sprouting. (The whites tend to come last for me.)

But on a windowsill in midwinter, a staggered progression is bliss over an extended period. And no catalog photo can convey the scent. Think Manischewitz wine with a double dose of cheap perfume drizzled with a hint of clove. In the case of 'Miss Saigon', multiply everything by ten. With 'Peter Stuyvesant', turn up the grape element in the configuration to Bacchus levels. No matter how you tweak the redolence, it doesn't come off as cloying in midwinter—at least, not to a hardened hyacinth hedonist.

Add the electrifying colors—magenta (my favorite being 'Miss Saigon'), deep midnight purple (as in 'Peter Stuyvesant'), or varying shades of blue (try 'Blue Jacket' or double navy 'Crystal Palace'), peach ('Gipsy Queen'), lipstick pink ('Jan Bos'), pale mango ('Odysseus'), or creamy yellow ('City of Haarlem')—and winter is suddenly all about seduction. The fact that these babies always seem to perform for Valentine's Day is wonderful compensation for all the nasty weather that also tends to coincide with that date.

You can't go wrong with hyacinths. They are all electrifying, and the scents are distinctly different but evocative (with the possible exception of 'Pink Elephant', which turned out to be underwhelming in both scent and performance). For pizzazz, they compete favorably with amaryllis, in a broader spectrum of colors. But no need to limit yourself. Do it all. Bombard your senses with bulbs.

Hyacinthus orientalis 'Crystal Palace' holds a thick, grape-like scent in every double purple flower.

Sound

THE SOUND OF SILENCE

I N THE BEGINNING, this property was pretty much a wall-to-wall tangle of poison ivy and brambles. There were no gardens, except a stray iris that survived despite decades of neglect and some stately trees that were undoubtedly vestiges of a long-ago attempt at wind barriers. Still, I pledged my allegiance to the property. I was dedicated to doing this seven-acre parcel proud. I made that commitment to the land, the spruces, and the sugar maple. The land and I had our first date in late autumn and I signed the papers in December, with no time to do anything besides a quick inventory of what to remove. At that point, masking the mess in a layer of nice clean snow was the best possible solution.

Now I value snow for a totally different reason. It protects the garden that slumbers beneath. The garden is negative space as well as plantings. It is paths and beds, fields and pastures, trees and the empty space between their trunks. It is the plantings and the projects not yet tackled or even imagined. The snow shields the entire scene from the plummeting temperatures and the biting winds. A lot of cruelty occurs in winter, and the snow serves as a humane barrier. Compared to the cacophony of winter's most dramatic histrionics, snow is a blessed relief. After the storm, who doesn't welcome the quiet?

You've heard it, I'm sure. More accurately, you haven't heard it. There is a pause after a snowstorm when everything just holds its breath. I'm talking about the sounds that don't echo the morning after the winds have wrought their havoc and worn out their vocal cords. You hear nothing at all at daybreak after we've been dumped on. Before the snowblowers come out in force, before the roads are reliably plowed, all of creation is gripped in a rare silence. A minor storm isn't sufficient to secure the lull. A dusting doesn't do it. Four inches is certainly an inconvenience (especially if you don't have a garage), but it halts nothing. A foot or more of snow must accumulate before the world is quieted. When it happens, that hush is almost worth dealing with the heaps of white stuff.

We become so accustomed to familiar sounds, we usually tune them out. Crows that caw do not cause anyone (except perhaps other crows) to stop in their tracks and take note. But if the world is suddenly stripped of those sounds, we notice their absence. No Canada geese hysterically announcing their descent, no chickadees fluttering around, no machines roaring away. You mark the quiescence. When it's just you and the shuffle, scrape, and plop of the snow shovel, you realize the layers you've been missing. But even the rhythm of your labor is stifled beneath a well-padded trooper's hat with earflaps. Despite the handicapping headgear, the total tranquility, the sense of unaccustomed quiet, is deafening.

Without distractions, the lure to listen becomes overwhelming. We desperately search for sounds to fill the void. We scan for the distant owl and the groan of ice on the pond. We fill in with our own soundtrack. We wait for the world as we know it to resume. Slowly, the audio returns.

The orchestra starts with the rhythm section. After the path is cleared, chores must be accomplished. The goats need their grain, warm water, some hay in their manger, and eventually another path shoveled so they can romp in their paddock (they are singularly spoiled goats). The simple crunch of my footfalls while going about these duties says everything. A well-shoveled path allows for an even step—no matter if it's to the car, to the newspaper (finding the paper is another story entirely), or for lugging buckets of water (and carrying sloshing water to livestock when the snow piles up adds a special level of tone to your biceps). Other sounds fill in. Gradually, the birds start to sound the all-clear. Flitting ensues. If the sun rises, all manner of tinkling, cracking, and dripping follows. Slowly, the machines rev up. A snowblower here, a plow truck there, a jet soaring overhead, and pretty soon the land's voice is overwhelmed by surround-sound. I will never admit to wishing for a major snowstorm. But there is beauty in its wake.

All is hushed after a storm, until the town starts moving into action again.

✳

THINGS THAT GO BOOM IN THE NIGHT

Many of winter's sounds will not be music to your ears, like the menacing howl as a gale force tosses tree limbs to the ground, the high-pitched squeal as an Arctic blast races around the corner of a wall, the scuttle of wind chasing twigs and the phantom squeaks it elicits. Winter is a vocal season. And none of it bodes well. The whistling sound that shrills when a microburst tries to muscle its way through the shed door evokes shivers. The creak as the fence is whipped back and forth keeps us pinned to the window in fearful anticipation that it might tumble down. When the crash comes after a gust has taken the game too far, we just don't want to hear about it. Most of winter's woes are signaled by sounds.

But not all of winter's acoustics spell disaster. Recently I was awoken from a deep winter slumber. It took a few moments to penetrate the fog of my dream state. Actually, it took another loud whoosh followed by an equally dramatic thud to tell me loud and clear that some sort of commotion was besieging the house. By the time my feet found the slippers, I figured out that I was witnessing the clatter of ice sliding off the greenhouse glass. What a relief!

Of all winter's refrains, snow rushing from glass or your roof is relatively welcoming. Sure, the melodramatic din always startles initially. It sounds uncomfortably akin to destruction. But this particular outburst is the clarion of good news. It means everything is going as planned. If the snow piles up on the glass or roof without fleeing, that could spell disaster. Although the noisy alternative will require a whole lot of shoveling action (with its inherent aches) when morning breaks, it is certainly preferable to the heart-rending smash of something breached overhead.

I've already padded downstairs (with Einstein leading the way) to check out the racket when the second avalanche gets under way. More

---

Keeping the snow from piling up on the greenhouse takes a lot of thermostat fiddling.
But when the new day dawns and the glass stands firm, it's golden.

sounds follow—welcome and not so delightful. I hear the sleet falling on naked glass; I turn on the outside light and see the piles mounting up. These are warning signals that demand action. I tally all the data, I consult with Intellicast, and I push the thermostat up a notch or two.

Pushing up the heat is my survival trick for greenhouse versus winter storm. When you live with a greenhouse, you learn that lesson fast. A winter storm is not the time to economize on heating bills. Keep the greenhouse temperatures warm (no lower than 60°F is my golden rule), never let a layer of ice accumulate, and wait for those telltale rumbles assuring that all will end well. At least we can get another few hours of shut-eye until the next clatter occurs. Snore, crash, dash, repeat. Welcome to winter in New England.

DRIP

A LOT OF LISTENING takes place indoors in winter, and it isn't confined to monitoring the battle cries of wind. Your indoor garden is expressing itself, too. Hear that gurgle? It's not the plumbing pipes or sleet slithering down windowpanes. That's the sound of water glugging down the sides of a terra-cotta container and into its saucer, eventually forming a nasty puddle on the floor. The whole mess started with a watering can servicing the houseplants. Actually, it was caused by reparations. You wouldn't hear that sound if all was going smoothly. But somehow, you skipped a watering. Okay, maybe more than one. The gurgle came when you tried to make amends. That drip is the cry of defeat when things are going terribly wrong with the soil.

That sound of the drip coming from the pedestal pot is never a good sign. I might be mopping up later.

Watering houseplants has a music all its own. It's the gush of water running into the watering can and the sprinkle as the flow is delivered to quench each plant's thirst. It is a science, starting with the search for the right watering can with just the right spout. Unfortunately, tool designers are rarely practitioners in the art of nurturing houseplants. They often design something that's visually appealing, but not necessarily practical. And watering cans meant for servicing the houseplant collection are designed differently than their outdoor cousins. It's not necessarily about transporting as much water as possible from the sink to the plant stands. You want a slender spout that delivers the goods precisely on target. Easy aim is crucial. And a slender spout prevents the water from flooding the recipient with an overly generous stream. Although it's tempting to lug around large watering cans with generous spouts to economize on trips back and forth to the sink, cleaning up the inevitable spills when the excess water slops onto the floor will take longer. You also want a can with a sufficiently ample mouth to be serviced by the faucet. My current romance is with a 2-liter Dramm. It has just the right ratio of spout length to reservoir capacity. The Haws has a long spout that is difficult for me to manipulate with the necessary precision, and the long nose can be an impediment when plants are clustered together. On the other hand, the long spout is perfect for plants that are out of easy reach. The Bloem 36-ounce cans are cute and do the job when you are delivering to only a houseplant or two. But they just don't hold enough water to keep 200-plus houseplants in business. (Don't ask about the houseplants unless you have a few hours to talk.)

The trick to watering is to do it consistently. You don't want to hear that gurgling, dripping sound. When potting soil becomes bone dry, it fails to take up water efficiently and its sponge action ceases to function properly. When you finally deliver water, the stream takes the easy route along the sides of the pot directly out the drainage hole without actually moistening the soil. The saucer fills up in a blink, it overflows, the furniture is ruined, and a puddle accumulates on the floor. You can usually hear it before you see it.

Water houseplants when the soil is slightly dry, but not parched. To cure the problem once it has occurred, fill a pan with water and let the plant drink it slowly from below. When the soil is properly moistened, the sponge action resumes and all is well.

Certain container shapes are more apt to rush water into the saucer too hastily. If you are a forgetful waterer, steer clear of containers with a large mouth contouring dramatically to a small base. Pedestal pots are prone to dripping. If the pedestal is hollow, the soil cannot slurp up excess water at its leisure, and you can't soak the plant from below. That's where I usually run into the disconcerting drip sound and the attendant puddles.

The best sound to hear when watering is no sound at all. Except for the possible swish of water coming through your spout and the steady trudge, trudge, trudge of your slippered feet shuffling back and forth from the sink, what you want is quiet.

Touch

BOGARTING SUNBEAMS

WHEN WINTER IS in full fury, the focus draws inward, especially when we're housebound. Outdoors is a nightmare: the brutal temperatures, the diabolical wind, the icy roads. But meanwhile, this morning dawned with gleaming sun, and now I'm jostling with Einstein for access to the sunbeams. Actually, it's a three-way competition between the resident furball (sometimes known as Big Squat), the 200 houseplants (for convenience, we'll think of them as a singular entity), and me.

And who can blame us if the elbowing gets nasty? There's nothing like a good, strong sunbeam in midwinter. Better than a heat vent, sunbeams are like a poultice. They reach out and touch your winter-hardened core. They massage your cracked, flaky skin. Sitting in the sun is mesmerizing; it's restful and restorative. Sunbeams lull you to sleep like a crackling fire on the hearth. They transport you back to summertime snoozes between weeding projects. But this is the guilt-free version. No carrot rows are calling to be thinned. No spirea needs to be whipped back into svelte shape with the shears. When digging holes is definitely not on the agenda and nothing could possibly be transplanted, you can enjoy the sun's rays with no pangs of remorse.

Are we agreed? You need all the sunbeams you can snag. So let's talk a minute about window treatments. I think they've gotten totally out of hand. Curtains have become so bulky that they allow just a tiny little sliver of sun to penetrate. And then folks whine about seasonal affective disorder. When light is scant in the winter, you need to be greedy. Take every single opportunity to nab a moment in the sun. It's good for the kitty, it's great for the houseplants, and you might be happier if you skipped some fabric and opted for a configuration that can be opened fully to let the sunshine in.

I recently began dressing my windows with curtains during the winter months in order to save energy. But if I don't open the insulating curtains immediately upon waking, Einstein is on my case. In his world, sunbeams are what the world is all about in winter. Even if it entails balancing on a pile of books or competing with the computer tower, he searches the

house relentlessly for sunbeam real estate. Sometimes it comes to fisti-cuffs, and that's where my houseplants become adversaries. If a geranium happens to be in the way, Einstein feels its demise is for a worthy cause. I'm more diplomatic. The south-facing window is sacred space for the cal-amondin orange, and I wouldn't displace its moment in the sun for the world. But it could move a little to the left, allowing me (or my feline side-kick) to snooze in a sunbeam.

Sunbeam real estate is like a jigsaw puzzle. Location, location, loca-tion. Stage the bromeliad behind the succulent and set the begonia on a low plant stand beneath the herbs—everyone spends the morning smil-ing. Evenly distributing the wealth is what indoor gardeners do in winter. Success is measured on how well you work the formula.

Domestic bliss for the entire family can be measured in foot-candles. But don't expect to bask in your victory for long. When you find your moment in the sun, it moves in a matter of minutes. But for a brief trea-sured interlude, everyone and everything can enjoy a perk that we take for granted (or even seek shelter from) in summer. Feel its warming fin-gers massaging your soul. Take turns, loll in the pleasure, and snooze with a friend—furry, green, or otherwise. I'm all about sharing.

REACH OUT AND TOUCH A LEAF

THERE'S MORE TO grasp in winter beyond just cold, hard reality. If you grow houseplants, you can pet your plants. Growing plants indoors is a whole different, more intimate relationship than cultivating plants outside. They really can become pets. Giving your plants a little pat every once in a while makes total sense. If you want to grow something that makes the experience more sensational, all the better.

Any plant that keeps Einstein from his sunbeams is imperiled.

I don't really select houseplants on the basis of their petability, but maybe I should. Instead, I usually think about textures and their visual interrelation. I also consider the containers and how they relate to the foliage. If you keep that in mind, you are bound to bring some wonderful leaf textures into the dialogue. Although I long ago decided that very thorny plants have no place in my happy home, plants that feel good are welcome.

I've already established my reputation for going beyond the obvious sanctioned houseplants that you can find labeled as such in garden centers (check out *The Unexpected Houseplant*). Keeping an open-door policy with houseplants expands the dialogue and brings the garden close by. This is one reason lamb's ears (*Stachys byzantina*) can frequently be found lounging on my windowsill. Grow it in a mini window box, and you are reminded of the summer garden. When the ground is frozen solid and everything is in deep slumber, you cherish that sort of association. It's not just about first glance; the leaves actually feel like the summer garden. Plain lamb's ears will do the trick, or you can go with one of the recent selections. Although 'Big Ears' isn't quite as plush as the species, 'Silver Carpet' brings the lamb analogy to another level.

Other refugees from the outdoor garden come inside, including *Salvia argentea*, which spends the dormant season making my life lovely on tactile and visual levels. It's virtually impossible to pass *S. argentea* without giving it a rub. The leaves are like a shag carpet. They actually resemble an old-man cactus (*Cephalocereus senilis*) without the nasty spines (you might want to skip that one for tactile purposes). Furthermore, various scented-leaf geraniums are sensational on many levels. Touch the leaves, give them a little rub, and wonderful scents float into the air thanks to the essential oils on the leaf surface. For petability as well as scent, one of the best is peppermint geranium, *Pelargonium tomentosum*. With glove-shaped leaves covered by a silvery felt, it tends to be a plush, plus-size plant. You can keep it in bounds by pruning frequently. Or go for 'Joy Lucille' (named for my mother-in-law), which is a hybrid between the peppermint- and rose-scented geraniums. It has velvety leaves, a wonderful scent, and it's more compact.

When you explore your indoor garden, there is no end to the touchy-feely experience. Beyond just furry leaves (which kids love), you

can reach out to your ferns and feel their pet-worthy fronds. Skip the asparagus ferns, which have barbs. Instead, run your fingers over velveteen plectranthus and get a thrill. Herbs such as mints and oreganos have intriguing textures, especially pineapple mint (*Mentha suaveolens* 'Variegata'). It adds another dimension to your life. Like all houseplants that engage your senses, these botanical roommates keep you out of trouble when digging into the dirt isn't a possibility. You know what they say about idle hands.

Salvia argentea, which feels like your favorite woolly blanket, is more easily petted when inside than in its usual position in the garden.

Taste

CITRUS

THE REFRIGERATOR IS well stocked and the freezer is bursting at its seams, but nonetheless you are hungry for something fresh and juicy. Because you are a gardener and you think like a gardener, you want to reach out and pluck something sweet and delectable and pop it straight into your waiting mouth. You want to look at something fresh and feel your saliva glands tingle in anticipation. Once you've tasted your own snacks, harvested from your own garden, you develop cravings that the supermarket simply cannot satisfy. And that's where citrus comes in.

Not all homegrown potted fruit is easy to host in your home. You might sprout an avocado, but the chances of harvesting fruit in your lifetime are slim. And good luck with the banana. A papaya fruiting in your living room would be heaven, but it's probably not going to happen. On the other hand, pomegranates are within your reach as an indoor gardener. And likewise, definitely, is the juicy goodness of citrus.

Although I would never claim that citrus is easy to grow, you can do it. Winter here is spent snacking blissfully on my calamondin orange (×*Citrofortunella microcarpa*), which sits in the brightest window I can manage. Of all the citrus, the calamondin orange is the easiest and most rewarding. You can pop this cross between a kumquat and a tangerine (presumably; I don't think they know its parentage for sure) into the mouth whole, rind and all. It might make you pucker and it's definitely tart, but you're courageous. And that fresh flavor burst—even if it tingles in your mouth—tastes so darn good in the middle of the winter.

Calamondin oranges produce their crop in abundance. Compared to the measly one or two treasured lemons you might eventually harvest on an indoor-grown lemon tree (*Citrus limon*) when it's finally sufficiently mature to support fruit, we're talking dozens of calamondins starting when plants are only 2 feet tall. Not long after the headily fragrant flowers appear in autumn, tiny calamondins start to develop, and the mere act of watching their progress should help stave off garden-withdrawal

symptoms. Plus, you often achieve a second crop of flowers in midwinter, resulting in more fruit. See what I mean about rewarding?

As for runners-up on Easy Street, if you can snag a kumquat, *Fortunella crassifolia* 'Meiwa' and *F. margarita* 'Nagami' are both abundant producers of fruit that you can pop into your mouth whole, although they aren't as easy to host as the calamondin. They tend to be finicky rather than robust. I've never tried growing a lime in my home, but I've listened to a lot of boasting from indoor gardeners who claim success with *Citrus aurantiifolia*, so it is possible. The Meyer lemon (*C. meyeri*) is also popular with windowsill gardeners. Fresh grapefruits, oranges, and citrons are more difficult to accomplish indoors.

How do you achieve indoor fruit? You'll need a sunny, south-facing window and nighttime temperatures that remain above 53°F with the thermometer rising warmer during the day. My citrus get a rich organic potting soil with compost included in the mixture. In fact, it's a good idea to shake off the sad soil in which the plant originally came to offer the roots something more nutritious. And give the plant a generous, but not huge, container. Instead, gradually repot in 2-inch graduations in size as the plant matures. Citrus tend to be thirsty plants, so remember to water them regularly. Take care to let the soil dry out slightly between waterings, but not to the point of being bone dry. If you are growing in a very dry environment, run a humidifier in the general vicinity of your citrus—it will be heaven for your sinuses as well. And fertilize your citrus, even during the winter. As an organic gardener both indoors and out, I use fish emulsion and serve it up once a month.

Nobody said that citrus were an easy fix, but they are definitely entertaining. As far as fruit goes, they are one of the only games in town during the winter, and successfully growing your own indoor harvest comes with plenty of bragging rights. For those of us who don't migrate south to Florida, they give our taste buds a little taste of sunshine.

The calamondin orange (×*Citrofortunella microcarpa*) is the easiest citrus to host in the average home.

ALL THAT GLITTERS

A FLURRY OF ACTIVITY caught the corner of my eye one midwinter morning. Something was afoot in the allée of beautyberry bushes (*Callicarpa dichotoma* 'Early Amethyst' and 'Issai') running along one side of my house. Further investigation revealed that the action was aerial. A crop mob of eastern bluebirds—all puffed up and four times their normal size—had descended for a fast and furious harvest. Like most feathered fly-ins, the party was over a few minutes after it began. But in that twinkling, the beautyberry allée was validated.

I planted the beautyberries for the benefit of birds. But the target audience largely ignored the potential feast of lavender-colored berries. Then, on a bitterly cold Valentine's Day morning after a subzero night, they came, hopping from rung to rung on a newly installed metal arbor that could support their weight, reaching over to pluck at berries borne on frail, wobbly, unstable branches. The callicarpa was the final dish on the menu, and there is still plenty of forage left on the branches. It probably wasn't dessert, but a last resort. But for a bird, disaster rations serve a critical function.

Plenty of food on the branch has proved more popular than the beautyberries. In fact, most berries don't even make it to winter. The race to the blueberries is tight. A lot of hungry mouths try to beat me to those plump, juicy morsels. By late summer, not a berry remains. Similarly, the currants and gooseberries are gone long before winter arrives (it's usually slim pickings by autumn). In the uncontested bird-fodder department, a buffet of various viburnums is available on premises, including *Viburnum sargentii* 'Chiquita', *V. lentago* (nannyberry), and *V. dilatatum* 'Henneke' (Cardinal Candy). True to name, Cardinal Candy disappears rapidly, whereas a much handsomer *V. dilatatum* 'Oneida' still has scads of extremely shriveled fruit left without takers through most of winter. A rowdy gang of robins that flew in one autumn day did not strip it, even after chasing off some smaller birds. Instead, the robins lost interest and flew off for further adventures, leaving plenty of unharvested fruit in their

wake. Gradually, as the berries become desiccated, the birds reluctantly peck away—it's the harvesting version of any port in a storm.

Birds have a split-second attention span. What keeps them more focused over the long haul is the winterberry (*Ilex verticillata*), which must freeze and thaw repeatedly before they show interest. Interestingly, it seems as though the orange and yellow types are the last to go. But the strip show occurs literally overnight. One day the shrubs are fully clothed, and the next they are naked.

Bluebirds are now all-season residents, dining on whatever berries they can find.

In a mild winter, the crop of unharvested winterberries might still be clinging sadly to the branches in spring. They are shriveled and battered, and have definitely seen better days. But that doesn't stop me from putting that berry on the menu. You never know when a frazzled little berry will spell the difference between life and death. That's food for thought.

DINING ON THE FLY

T HE SAME ROWDY gang of robins that hit the berries blew into town when winter was almost a done deal. This time, they were swaggering around with the juncos. The feathered version of a flash mob, they swooped into town the moment warm rain left bare ground. Who knows how they get the word, but they are definitely on the ball. A stray cardinal and a couple of blue jays joined the cleanup crew as a randomly choreographed pandemonium of scratching and pecking in the soft spots between the iris, spirea, and physocarpus ensued. They proceeded with the energetic unearthing. They did a little socializing, and apparently there was enough for everyone. And then they moved on to browner pastures.

The beauty of flocks is they all seem to socialize seamlessly in winter. Summer might be a different story. And crows are never invited to the party (they throw their own wingdings). But in winter, almost anything goes. Desperate times lead to peaceful coexistence.

One of the best things you can do for the tufted titmice and dark-eyed juncos is rake leaves. At least, that's what I found after cleaning up along the woods line of my property. The area hadn't been raked in years, but it's next up for a face-lift. So when a January thaw left bare ground, I was ready with my rake. A day later, the juncos saw the opportunity to further excavate the future planting site, and they have been tidying up ever since. Fingers crossed that a few ticks have been ingested as snacks in the process—birds are such efficient disposal units.

While the flock was fluttering around, they paid a visit to the upper herb and vegetable beds. We all know that deer eat more than their fair daily ration of kale. But dark-eyed juncos also indulge. They might be eating aphids or another insect off the leaves because their delicate little nibbles did no detectable damage. If so, they're hired to patrol the kale on an annual basis. (That's another argument for bringing in the flight crew—they support the health of the crop rather than mar it.) The kale in question was 'Redbor', and the frozen, brittle leaves spaced far apart

A chickadee checks out the cafeteria from its perch.

on this table-bred vegetable (compared to the ornamental versions with closely stacked foliage) provided the landing pad. The elongated stripped stem that developed after a year's growth served as the perfect perch.

The moral here is that birdfeeders are not the only option. Of course, after a snowstorm, a nice dry perch and a feeder on a tall pole is luxury dining for birds, but they make full use of what's available in the garden as well. Work together with nature, and everyone is nurtured.

FINALE

Forcing the Issue

O F COURSE, all of this goes full circle. Just because the seasons turn over doesn't mean we aren't attentive to past perks and watching vigilantly for forthcoming sensations. Whether it's birdsong or violent storms, we're on the lookout and we're listening. Wind and its music serenade us throughout the year, be it March winds or autumn gales. And we can always come up with an excuse to plunge our hands in the mud, no matter what the calendar is reading timewise. Being present for the magic of each season is what we've been sharpening in these pages, but there is always homogeneity. Undoubtedly you've noticed the considerable cross-pollination back and forth between sensations striking you on many levels. It was always a debate whether I should talk about wind for its touch or sound. In the same way, the seasons also flow one into the next.

In winter, gardeners are apt to think ahead. At other times of year, maybe we don't push it. Endless summer would be fine with most gardeners, as we loll in its gifts. On the other hand, winter is the dark horse. As much as there is to savor in winter, who doesn't thirst for spring? So a little sneak into the sensations of spring while still in the depths of winter wouldn't be a bad thing, no? At an interval when there is pretty much solid white outdoors and your days are spent huddling inside with the houseplants, a little hope would be welcome. Let nature bridge the seasons. Cheat winter without bailing to the Bahamas. Remind your senses of forthcoming perks. Try a little subterfuge.

Find your way to a forsythia or pussy willow (or just pick up some pussy willows at a flower show) and bring them in. Shovel a path to your budded *Cornus mas* (or in my case, its lookalike *C. officinalis*) and swipe a few branches (neither of those plants will ever miss them). It's equally apropos for magnolias, flowering cherry, redbud, you name it. Fetch them inside, put them in a vase, and wait. Display them where you most thirst to see some nature inside. Put them where even a few hopeful branches might quench your cravings for flowers, and watch. Because magic is about to occur.

Your sense of sight is the obvious beneficiary. Before they even burst open, just having the warp and woof of budded branches stretching their limbs inside is going to blur the lines between indoors and out. Whenever you walk through the door into that room, those branches are going to greet you with the open arms of the outdoors. You're going to remember walks in the woods. You're going to think ahead to the upcoming garden performance of your *Viburnum carlesii* even though it's currently half-buried in a snowbank. And maybe you won't be so homesick for nature.

Maybe gardening is about fiddling with fate. Perhaps gardening is about putting yourself into the action. This is Act V in the theatrics of being cognizant of nature. It's a way to hone your senses when you have time. The moment is everything. And all your senses are the benefactors. Those magnolia buds are like velveteen in your fingers. That Korean spice viburnum emits a perfume second to none. With all your honed skills and perceptions, you can play this moment for all its worth. And that's what these pages are all about.

If this becomes a midseason ritual, nobody can blame you. If forsythias are as much a part of your winter as they are a facet of spring, then hooray for you. And if you tarry just a moment longer than usual to truly see that flower, this is yet another victory in your awakening. This book is about how you come to link with your land on all levels, however you can make that happen. It is very individual, it is very deep, and it can mean the world.

Please forgive me if I neglected to mention your favorite sensation or if you perceive it differently. The scent I describe in summer might not match your experience. The way a storm hits me or how a tool works in my hands may not be the same for you. Go ahead, take issue with me. Grumble to yourself that I've gotten something all wrong. Go to my

---

Although they are precocious outside, a few cut branches of *Cornus officinalis* make all the difference forced in a vase.

Facebook page (tovah martin at plantswise) and tell me I'm all wet. I'd love to hear from you. What I'm asking you to do is just plug in and see, sniff, hear, feel, savor for yourself. And keep on comprehending. Grasp and take in. Inhale and define. Work that garden for all it is worth, because it is worth the world. Take that place you've fashioned, fully explore its potential, and you will learn. You will learn about nature by stewarding it. You will learn about the earth from holding it. You will know the good and the bad and the indifferent of the never-ending cycles. So go out and grow with your landscape, become its confidante. This dialogue is to be continued. The pages of this narrative will never stop turning. Once you engage with your garden in all senses, it's a union forever. So stay attuned.

Now go out and write your own script.

ACKNOWLEDGMENTS

Any awakening owes its aha moment to a crowd of influences. This book never would have happened without a whole lot of friends and fellow gardeners reminding me to slow down and breathe in. I thank you all. One friend in particular showed me the way: Lee May, I wish you could have remained with us to see this book be born. In addition to insight, I have friends to thank for sharing their wisdom. In particular, I would like to thank Sydney Eddison, Ray Belding, Tricia van Oers, Benjamin Pauly of The Woodstock Inn, Toddy Benivegna, Michael Marriott of David Austin Roses, Sally Ferguson, and Phil Forsyth of the Philadelphia Orchard Project. James Baggett, you are an inspiration and guiding light. And where would I be without the friends who stopped by and helped with garden chores that proved too massive for me to tackle alone? Denny Sega and Rob Girard, you are saints.

Many people joined together to assist in the making of this book. For juggling thousands of photos with the greatest of ease, Jody Hall was brilliant. At Timber Press, Tom Fischer and Andrew Beckman steered this book into its current guise—thank you for your insights. Mike Dempsey, Eve Goodman, and Sarah Rutledge sweated the details and smoothed the words. Patrick Barber and the design team made this book beautiful. But most of all, my sincere gratitude and a huge hug to Kindra Clineff, who shared the vision for this book and guided it from its formative stages onward to fruition. Kindra's perceptive and visual talents uplifted this project. Every photo she composes is accomplished with imagination, creativity, and courage to go beyond the obvious. She is an inspiration, a dream collaborator, and a dear friend.

INDEX

© Kindra Clineff

TOVAH MARTIN woke up one morning, looked at her seven-acre Connecticut garden, and realized that she wasn't grasping its full sensory potential. That's when the awakening began. Tovah is a fanatical and passionate organic gardener, and the author of *Tasha Tudor's Garden*, as well as many other gardening books. Her articles appear in a broad range of magazines and periodicals, including *Country Gardens*, *Garden Design*, *Coastal Home*, *Martha Stewart Living*, and *Gardens Illustrated*, and she lectures extensively throughout the country. What she loves most is linking with fellow gardeners. To share how you experience your own garden in all senses, join her on Facebook at Plantswise by Tovah Martin and take part in the ongoing discussion. For more information on her whereabouts, go to tovahmartin.com.

© Tovah Martin

KINDRA CLINEFF travels far and wide specializing in location photography for commercial and editorial clients. She regularly produces feature assignments for national magazines, and her images have appeared in numerous books. Kindra also collaborated with Tovah Martin on her recent books, *The Indestructible Houseplant*, *The Unexpected Houseplant*, and *The New Terrarium*. When not chasing light, Kindra can be found cultivating heirloom vegetables and attempting to tame the perennial garden of her seventeenth-century home in Essex County, Massachusetts.

To my father, in loving memory

Published in 2018 by Timber Press, Inc.
The Haseltine Building
133 S.W. Second Avenue, Suite 450
Portland, Oregon 97204-3527
timberpress.com

Printed in China
Cover design by Mia Nolting
Text design by Laura Shaw Design
Illustrations by Nina Montenegro

Library of Congress Cataloging-in-Publication Data

Names: Martin, Tovah, author. | Clineff, Kindra, photographer.
Title: The garden in every sense and season / Tovah Martin; photographs by
    Kindra Clineff.
Description: Portland, Oregon: Timber Press, 2018. | Includes index.
Identifiers: LCCN 2017046295 (print) | LCCN 2017049591 (ebook) | ISBN
    9781604698596 | ISBN 9781604697452 (hardcover)
Subjects: LCSH: Horticultural literature. | Gardening. | Essays.
Classification: LCC SB318.3 (ebook) | LCC SB318.3 .M37 2018 (print) | DDC 635–
    dc23
LC record available at https://lccn.loc.gov/2017046295

A catalog record for this book is also available from the British Library.